AF255797

"In *Boundary-Breaking Mission*, Simone Twibell addresses in a concise and readable manner not only historic questions but also current issues seldom included in typical mission texts. Readers will be challenged and their horizons for ministry expanded."

—**CRAIG OTT**, professor of mission and intercultural studies, Trinity Evangelical Divinity School

"Engaging, timely, hopeful! Simone Twibell's *Boundary-Breaking Mission* is a fresh take on the contemporary challenges of the worldwide Christian mission. Twibell tackles oft neglected issues of Western individualism, the 'spirit' world, influences of the digital revolution, the 'nones' and the poor, and the church's relationship to other religions, but does so with her unique boundary-breaking blend of South American and female insights. This is a book that I will delightfully highlight in my upcoming teaching cycles."

—**FLETCHER L. TINK**, director of the PhD program in transformational development, Asia Graduate School of Theology

"Disruption. Few words can better describe the current context of Western missiology. Simone Twibell invites readers to wrestle with the impacts of disruption within traditional loci of social capital, the increasing disassociation from organized religion, and the impact of globalism. With little interest in remedying the challenges, Twibell locates the possibility of the church's witness within a robust missional framework, inviting readers to recognize the opportunities of holistic transformation and friendship."

—**JEFF STARK**, associate professor of Christian ministry, Olivet Nazarene University

"Simone Twibell locates the challenges the Western church must navigate to bear witness from the margins to a turbulent world amidst the increasing cultural, religious, and social currents of multiculturalism, pluralism, and polarization. If you're looking for a text at the intersection of missiological, sociological, and theological reflection from a rising scholar on historical and theological perspectives of mission and witness that moves the project forward, this is it."

—**BETH SEVERSEN**, author of *Not Done Yet: Reaching and Keeping Unchurched Emerging Adults*

"*Boundary-Breaking Mission* is a book on mission for our time. Simone Twibell offers us an expansive view of mission, one that is theologically grounded, attuned to contemporary contexts like the digital age and a multireligious world, and big enough to embrace the full range of human needs. It addresses issues like witness to the 'nones' and spiritual warfare that aren't always included in mission texts. This small book packs a punch! I encourage students, pastors, missionaries, and people engaged in God's mission to read and learn from it."

—**DEAN FLEMMING**, professor emeritus of New Testament and missions, MidAmerica Nazarene University

Boundary-Breaking Mission

Boundary-Breaking Mission

The Gospel in a Diverse and Fragmented World

Simone Mulieri Twibell

WIPF & STOCK · Eugene, Oregon

BOUNDARY-BREAKING MISSION
The Gospel in a Diverse and Fragmented World

Wipf & Stock
An Imprint of Wipf and Stock Publishers
199 W. 8th Ave., Suite 3
Eugene, OR 97401

www.wipfandstock.com

PAPERBACK ISBN: 978-1-6667-5769-9
HARDCOVER ISBN: 978-1-6667-5770-5
EBOOK ISBN: 978-1-6667-5771-2

08/02/23

To my parents, Alfredo and Rute Mulieri, for modeling the rhythms of faithful living in the margins, and to Renee Twibell, who has walked with me with undeniable love at the margins.

Contents

Acknowledgments

Writing a book is no easy task. Many hours go into research and writing. It has been said that it takes a village to raise a child, and the same could be said about writing a book. For the encouragement, understanding, and faithful prayers of my village at Olivet Nazarene University who fostered the type of environment I needed to write this book, I will be forever grateful. This book could not have become a reality without the generous support provided by the Craighton T. and Linda G. Hippenhammer Faculty Scholarship Fund.

My children, Lucas and Sofia, have patiently understood when I could not play as often as we would have liked during the many months of extra hours in the office. To Renee Twibell, my mother-in-law, who spent countless hours with my children so that I could devote time to writing, I will be forever grateful. Bruce Barron, editor of the *Evangelical Review of Theology* journal, read an early draft of the manuscript and offered helpful insights. Most substantially, I am deeply appreciative of the many people of God who have contributed to the ongoing discourse on the mission of the church. I hope that I can offer a useful addition to this discussion.

Preface

The perspectives set forth in this book have been shaped by many years of study as well as by my personal experiences. My approach to the doctrine of the church and its mission has been informed by years of both formal theological education and practical ministry. My pastoral work included ten years of service in two local churches as both associate and senior pastor. In addition, I grew up on the mission field in South America and participated as a volunteer missionary in Central America. Finally, my current assignment as assistant professor of Intercultural Studies and Missions at Olivet Nazarene University in Illinois has deepened my skills and foundational knowledge, bringing me to the point where I felt I could make a useful book-length contribution to this field.

My desire to learn about and know God has marked my life journey since my early years. After earning my first master's degree at Olivet Nazarene University, I taught myself Greek in order to pass the language entrance exam at Asbury Theological Seminary, where I obtained my Master in Divinity. My PhD studies at Trinity International University in the field of Intercultural Studies expanded my knowledge of the nature and mission of the church. My doctoral dissertation focused on researching global partnerships with a particular view on the impact and effect of reverse short-term missions (RSTM) and I was selected as a Waybright scholar to complete my studies. The preparation of my mind through rigorous study has certainly helped to shape the perspectives described here. However, mental preparation alone is not enough. The preparation of the heart and the spirit by responding to the grace of God through prayer in its many forms, as described in my previous book, *Intimacy with God*, has also contributed to the insights shared in this book.

Along with the many opportunities and accomplishments that life brings, weaknesses and frailties are inevitable aspects of our human experience. I write this book cognizant of my current contextual realities. I have needed extra effort and inner strength to carry out this project while mourning the death of my husband, raising two small children, and teaching full-time. My completion of this book has truly been a sign of God's grace. I often wondered if I would be able to finish it at all. But the continual encouragement that my community offered along the way and the subtle voice of the Spirit propelling me forward enabled me to cross the finish line. The reassurances offered by my community were never interpreted as a mere act of kindness. Rather, they became God's own invitation to pause and reflect on his love as expressed through the love of his people. Likewise, our encounters with those in our society are God's creative offer to become fully immersed in the love of the Christ whom we may find hidden in the faces of our neighbors. To him, who is most visible in the obscurity of the margins, be all glory for all eternity.

Introduction

Postmodernity has influenced multiple areas of contemporary life and thought, having been the subject of reflection in philosophy, ethics, aesthetics, and most clearly at the cultural level. The postmodern condition has required the church to reconsider its priorities and rethink its witness in our surrounding culture. How should we preach Christ and bear witness to the gospel in a postmodern world? How do we navigate the turbulent waters of social, cultural, and religious difference in a pluralistic society? How do we minister effectively in multicultural contexts and find ways to swim against the unconscious currents of ethnocentrism? This book seeks to address these questions. But since the world in which we live is both complex and fragmented, the answers we might find plausible today will continually need to be revisited tomorrow.

The church in the West has been living in exile for quite some time, and it may have to grow accustomed to the fact that its position will remain in the margins, at least for the foreseeable future. Even when the prognosis seems dire, the marginalization of the church in the West may not be as drastic as it appears. The current situation of the church may actually be considered a "strategic crisis."[1] This position may lead the church to reevaluate its priorities, refocus its vision, and redirect its missional efforts ever more clearly to reach individuals with a message of hope. The language of exile is not a new way to describe the state of the

---

1. Williams, *Exiles on Mission*, xv.

church in the West[2] and proposals to clarify the mission of the church keep appearing,[3] but often missing from such discourse is an integrative approach that considers sociological trends that are guided by theological and missiological reflection to address these contextual realities in practical ways. I have written this book with the goal of calling the church to embrace intentional forms of witness to our neighbors whose religious views, socio-economic levels, cultural backgrounds, and life experiences differ from ours to various degrees.

The complexities of our world call for different approaches in evangelism, and the way in which we bear witness to the gospel needs to be contextualized to the many different people groups we encounter along the pathway of life. Rick Allbee writes, "Christian disciples today, like the early church, need to be deeply concerned with witnessing to their neighbor and with witnessing also to their neighbor's culture by living out their own loving kingdom ethic in everyday life."[4] This unique witness offers the church an opportunity to display its *raison d'être,* which is to continue the witness and mission that Christ inaugurated when he came to earth.

I have divided this book into three sections to explore Christ's all-encompassing mission in which we are called to participate. Part I explores what it means to be the people of God as the extension of Christ in the world. It would be remiss to delve into an analysis of the church's mission without first discussing how and why our missionary God has called the church to accomplish his mission. The church cannot redirect its attention to reach people in a changing world without first focusing on the Person who made it possible for the church to embark on such efforts. When the very foundation of the church is imperiled by external factors and its effective witness is hindered by a lack of proper grounding, the church must go back to its roots. A rediscovery of the church's nature and purpose in the world will help the church embrace a

2. See Paul Williams, *Exiles on Mission* for further reflection.

3. See Craig Ott, *The Mission of the Church* for a concise historical development of the understandings of the mission of the church.

4. Allbee, "Christ Witnessing," 31.

more robust, consistent, and vibrant mission. The church of Jesus Christ must remain dependent on the grace of God and become more fully aware of the work of the Spirit in order to move with intentionality in its contemporary context.

Part II describes the complexities and cultural shifts in our constantly changing world and how this reality calls for a redesign of our witness that emphasizes amicable interaction with our surrounding world. Technological platforms have created new opportunities for engagement, and religious trends keep challenging the church to think anew about its mission. Thus, this section describes the ways in which we can become witnesses primarily through friendship, hospitality, and dialogue. The complexities surrounding gender and identity issues, which also call for missiological reflection, are not covered here, because they cannot easily be addressed in a single chapter. That topic deserves its own treatment, which is beyond the scope of this book to undertake but which other excellent Christian writers have taken on.[5]

Part III addresses forms of holistic mission that focus on physical, emotional, and spiritual factors that can interfere with people's sense of well-being. This section takes into consideration the pressing problem that the poor, the immigrants, the oppressed, and the broken seem to be increasing not only in number but also increasing in need. My goal is to provide theological principles that build on the research that has guided discussions of holistic mission up to this point. I have added a chapter describing the reality of the spirit world, which has traditionally been missing from discussions of holistic ministry. The Western church has much to learn about suffering, hardship, and pain—issues that have long affected other parts of the world. Illnesses, poverty, mental health issues, family disintegration, and the continual influx of immigrants have challenged the church to think anew about what it means to minister in

---

5. Several biblical and theological presentations have appeared recently to address the topic of gender dysphoria and sexual orientation. Among the most recent and leading experts are Timothy Tennent, *For the Body* (2021); Mark Yarhouse and Olya Zaporozhets, *Costly Obedience* (2019); Christopher Yuan, *Holy Sexuality and the Gospel* (2018); Beth Felker Jones, *Faithful: A Theology of Sex* (2015); and Robert Gagnon, *The Bible and Homosexual Practice* (2002).

a fragmented world. Amidst this diversity and in the middle of brokenness, such an examination promises a rekindling of prophetic imagination to participate ever more fully in the mission of God.

Pope Francis captured this opportunity when he stated, "The church is called upon to come out of itself and go to the margins, not only geographical, but also in human terms, where the mystery of sin, pain, injustice, and ignorance dwells, where there is contempt for religious and for religious thinking and where there are all kinds of misery."[6] It is there, where mystery and misery meet, that the church might find a renewed sense of purpose and impetus to bear witness to the good news of Jesus Christ in a world that thirsts for living waters. Samuel Escobar reminds us that mission includes compassion as well as confrontation. Compassion arises as a result of our involvement with people whose need requires intentional effort and interventions. Confrontation takes place when systems that oppress groups of people are challenged and disarmed. Escobar affirms that "Jesus' mission becomes a fertile source of inspiration, because it contains the seeds of new patterns being explored today through practice and reflection, patterns involving a simple lifestyle, holistic mission, the unity of the church for mission, God's kingdom as a missiological paradigm, and spiritual conflict."[7]

Because the mission of the church is fostered and strengthened by the rhythms of the Spirit, we can rest assured that his plans for the restoration of all things will never be thwarted. Yet in another sense, because the church is the means by which the Spirit carries out the work of the Kingdom, the Lord desires to partner with us in this endeavor. This beautiful relationship reminds us that God's plans for the church are in his hands and will ultimately prevail. The Spirit who gave birth to the church through the Christ event is always working in and moving through the church. Hope is the fountain of life and life is lived in the rivers of God's grace in relationship with others; therefore, we should always keep in mind that the Spirit of God, who gives us such hope, is leading the way.

6. Quoted in Riccardi, *Margins*, 2.

7. Escobar, *The New Global*, 107.

Part I

Recovering the Essentials

1

The Missionary God

THE SCRIPTURES REVEAL THE story of a God who is on a mission of restoration. At creation, God's plan of redemption was already an ever-present reality in his mind—specifically, that if the human race broke fellowship with the Spirit, this would require the sending of the Son, through his death and resurrection, to enact God's cosmic plan of redemption. This chapter describes how our missionary God planned to redeem the world from its brokenness by ultimately sending his Son on a mission of rescue.

The Journey to Redemption

The Spirit of God has been at work since the beginning of creation. We find the Father, the Son, and the Spirit sharing in the work of creation. Whereas the Father does all the speaking, the Spirit does all the moving, and the Son seems to do all the listening. Creation could not have been possible without this partnership. When God saw that the earth was formless and empty, he began to create *ex nihilo*—out of nothing: "In the beginning God created the heavens and the earth. Now, the earth was formless and empty, darkness was over the surface of the deep, and the Spirit of God was hovering over the waters" (Gen 1:1). The words "formless" and "empty" are the Hebrew words *tohu* and *bohu,* which render the idea of something meaningless, without purpose. The world was not in a state of chaos *per se*; it was in a state of emptiness and void.

The Spirit moved at the Father's command to bring forth something out of nothing. When God said, "Let there be light," the Spirit, the bond of love and unity, made it possible for light to appear. Through the activation of God's voice and the movement of his Spirit, elements began to appear. As they appeared, they were separated. This separation was important because it could give way to an appropriate filling. When all the elements God spoke into existence were separated, God filled the earth and blessed it. Just as at creation, the Spirit of God still hovers over the earth and moves in a unique way to bring about God's purposes on earth. He moves from the particular to reach the universal. In fact, the Scriptures reveal this pattern as God selects individuals to fulfill a unique purpose or mission, giving them the promise of his guidance while blessing others through them, all with the intention to restore God's creation.

God's redemptive purpose in salvation history reached its climax in the sending of Christ, but it began with the calling of Noah and was more specifically revealed through Abraham. The calling of Abraham represents the theological hinge between the reality of sin and the beginning of grace. His calling in Gen 12:1–4 has been called a "bridge-passage,"[1] which serves as a link between the first eleven chapters and the rest of the book. The first section (Gen 1–11) shows the devastation and failure of sin, pictured through the fall of Adam and Eve, the Flood, and the Tower of Babel. The second section (Gen 12–50) describes the history of the patriarchs and the formation of the people of Israel. Just as Adam's sin resulted in consequences and curses for the land, Abraham and his obedience brought about the opportunity for the Spirit of God to restore the land.

The calling of Abraham is crucial to understand the nature and purpose of the community God formed through the patriarchs. Abraham was not chosen because of his abilities or his perfect obedience. On the contrary, he was chosen as a representative

---

1. Wolff, "Kerygma of the Yahwist," 136.

of the human race to be a vehicle of blessing to many, and this was God's own choosing. Michael Goheen notes, "Blessing is a biblical term with rich resonances, implying the reversal of sin's curse and the restoration of creation's fullness."[2] It is not related to the popular and cultural assumption that God will endow us with health and wealth at every point and grant every wish simply because we are "blessed." On the contrary, the blessing of God is much more sustaining, showing the way in which the Spirit journeys with us to redeem that which was tainted by sin and remains in need of full restoration.

A Covenantal Community

The Spirit moves from the particular to the universal to accomplish his purposes, not just through the particular callings of individuals but also through entire communities and nations. Through the formation of the people of Israel, God called a group of people to be a light unto the nations. The called people of God were brought into covenant with him and selected not for "superiority but for service."[3] Thus, the election of God's people is not to be understood as a *select* group but as a *selected* people. The Israelites were to embody God's redemptive blessings by walking in covenantal relationship with God so that the nations around them might come to know God also.

The nation of Israel that issued from Abraham was chosen to participate as a vehicle of the blessing of God, as bearers of his *shalom*, and as a sign of hope and light throughout the surrounding nations. They were to embody God's redemptive blessing by walking in the way of the Lord so that the nations might come to enjoy the blessing of God. God desired to form and nurture a community that would be the bearers of his glory and attract others to him. The very idea of God's mission in the Old Testament was possible because of the gravitational force of his Spirit, who drew

2. Goheen, *A Light to the Nations,* 31.

3. Oden, *Classic Christianity,* 532.

individuals together to form a community that would fellowship and covenant with him.

In the book of Exodus, the redemption of God's people is presented through the calling of Moses and the establishment of a covenant with the entire nation of Israel. God heard Israel's groaning in slavery and remembered his covenant with Abraham to bless his people. The redemption that led the people out of slavery had political, economic, social, and religious implications. This redemption was all-encompassing. It did not refer solely to the eternal salvation of a group of people; rather, it pointed to the need for political liberation from corrupt systems as well as spiritual deliverance from oppressive forces of evil. The people of Israel were living in darkness, oppressed by the tyrannical rule of Pharaoh. Amidst their groans and desperation, God activated his voice once again and called a deliverer to lead the redeemed community into their true identity—a covenantal community.

For Israel to fulfill their calling to the nations, forgiveness, commitment, and fellowship with God were essential. The identity markers of the nation of Israel indicate their special role in God's overarching plan to reach the nations so that those nations would also enjoy and share in this identity. Exodus 19:3–6 describes the characteristics of the people God was raising up to serve as a means by which his presence would be manifested and made known to the rest of the nations: "Now if you obey me fully and keep my covenant, then out of all nations you will be my treasured possession. Although the whole earth is mine, you will be for me a kingdom of priests and a holy nation." This promise was conditional: *if* they kept the covenant, they would be a treasured possession. God chose Israel as the first fruits, the means by which the other nations would come to know what he was like by virtue of seeing how God cared for Israel. God also said he intended for them to be a kingdom of priests. Priests were called to mediate the presence of God to the rest of the people, intercede for the community, and make confession on behalf of the people. They were to act as mediators between God and sinners, which was only possible if they were set apart in holiness. And that is why the people of Israel were to be a *holy nation.* Israel was called into this role as a nation for the sake of the other nations. Israel was given plenty of freedom to obey God's commands, but ultimately they failed to live up to God's vision.

Hopeful Signs in Dark Times

Even though Israel failed to live up to their calling as a holy people, God promised to provide the means by which they might fulfill their calling once again. During their darkest time as a stateless minority scattered among the nations, God did not leave them without signs of hope; instead, he raised up prophets to encourage, exhort, and challenge the remnant living in exile. Here we find the Spirit moving once again, in the midst of darkness, to bring about the purposes of God.

In the middle of what seemed to be the most excruciating and devastating time in the life of the nation of Israel, God did not leave himself without witness. Recognizing the people's sheer inability to keep his covenant and follow his commandments, God promised to make a new covenant with his people that would enable them to fulfill his law from the inside out. God spoke through the prophet Jeremiah: "This is the covenant I will make with the people of Israel after that time. I will put my law in their minds and write it on their hearts. I will be their God, and they will be my people" (Jer 31:33). The law would be fulfilled through an internal disposition rather than an external obligation.

Even when the Israelites failed to keep their end of the bargain, God remained faithful and provided another way by which the people of God would be able to fulfill their calling. Through the new covenant, his people would be enabled to carry out their mission. That new covenant was made possible by the coming of God himself in the person of Christ. Through the sending of Jesus, a new community would be brought into existence to serve the purposes of God's Kingdom in the world. The church would be called to embrace and live into its true identity as a chosen people and a kingdom of priests: "But you are a chosen people, a holy nation, God's special possession, that you may declare the praises of him who called you out of darkness into his wonderful light" (1 Pet 2:9). The same identity markers previously given to Israel were now spoken to the church, composed of Jews and Gentiles, women and men, free people and slaves. Their calling was linked to their identity. The true "light of life" was coming down to earth (John 8:12) so that the church would carry his torch to all humanity as the "light of the world" (Matt 5:14).

Let There Be Light!

Jesus was the true light that gave light to the whole world (John 1:9). When we think about Jesus and his role in salvation history, we must first understand his character. Why would he embark on a journey to redeem a broken world? Why would he leave his glory behind and come in the form of a baby? Perhaps because he was the only giver of life and the only One who could rescue people out of darkness. When we consider the role of Jesus as Savior in the economy of God's redemptive plans, two distinct appellations illumine his identity. He is the *Lion* of Judah who conquers death (Rev 5:5) and the *Lamb* of God who takes away the sins of the world (John 1:29; Rev 5:6). Jonathan Edwards, inspired by the imagery in Revelation chapter 5, wrote a sermon titled *The Excellency of Christ* where he captured this binary with the following words:

> There is an admirable conjunction of diverse excellencies in the Person of Jesus Christ. The lion and the lamb, though very diverse kinds of creatures, yet have each their peculiar excellencies. The lion excels in strength, and in the majesty of his appearance and voice: the lamb excels in meekness and patience, besides the excellent nature of the creature as good for food, and yielding that which is fit for our clothing and being suitable to be offered in sacrifice to God. But we see that Christ is in the text compared to both, because the diverse excellencies of both wonderfully meet in him.[4]

4. Edwards, "The Excellency of Christ," 2.

In other words, in Christ we see infinite power and genuine humility, infinite justice and undeniable grace. He is a solid rock, and he is also the living bread. Jesus Christ combines character traits that seem opposed to each other, but they come together perfectly in him. His earthly ministry is also marked by these binaries. He is compassionate toward the needy and harsh toward the proud. He forgives sinners and challenges systems. He is merciful and he is zealous. He is both a lion and a lamb.

The Living Gospel

Central to the gospel message is the idea that God has revealed his presence in Christ, who took on human flesh and dwelt among a people. In 1 Timothy 3:16, we find a testimony to the early church's understanding of the second person of the Trinity entering into human flesh:

> He appeared in the flesh,
> was vindicated by the Spirit,
> was seen by angels,
> was preached among the nations,
> was believed on in the world,
> was taken up in glory.

This hymn functions as a short creed, offering a brief overview of the life of Christ, which begins in the incarnation, as he "appeared in the flesh," and culminates in his ascension, when he was "taken up in glory." It is thus logical to turn our attention to yet another paradoxical conjunction—his divine essence and human nature.

The transcendental reality of Christ as God and his immanence has not always been interpreted correctly. The long series of debates on this question that have raged since the early church reminds us that a wide range of views have emerged across two thousand years of church history. Ecumenical councils from the beginning of church history, such as the Council of Nicaea, developed creeds not only to summarize the essential beliefs of the Christian faith, but also to combat heresies that were emerging.

One of the early debates centered on the identity of Christ and whether he was *homoousios* (of the same substance as God) or *homoiousios* (of similar substance). Patristic consensus opted for the former in an effort to counteract the subordinationism of Arius and declared that the divine nature shared by the Father, the Son, and the Holy Spirit was coequal and consubstantial.

The double nature of Jesus, as fully human and fully divine, is evidenced in two of his declarative statements: "Anyone who has seen me has seen the Father" (John 14:9); "Truly, truly I tell you, before Abraham was, I am" (John 8:58). To see Christ in human flesh is to see God divested of his all-consuming power through the volitional choice to humble himself. God's essential nature is revealed in the person of Christ. In other words, to see Christ in human flesh is to see the extent of God's love for humanity. For Christ, taking on human flesh meant making himself nothing, taking the very nature of a servant, and leaving his glory behind (Phil 2:6–9). Sharing in human nature meant that God would suffer at the hands of the very people he came to rescue (Heb 2:14), and that he would invite persecution, the normal state of committed Christians in this day and age.

Christ's incarnation reveals several implications. First, embedded in the incarnation is a deep *identification* with humanity. Jesus came to identify with broken, sinful humanity as he learned submission and obedience by what he suffered (Heb 5:8). He truly identified with the lowly, the outcast, and the poor. Jesus identified with common people as the son of a carpenter and a young maiden. He also identified with those who endure hardship, as he was a man acquainted with sorrow, weaknesses, and pain (Isa 53:3; Heb 4:15).

Second, the incarnation is not only about identification; it also illustrates the action of *translation*, or a process of relocation from one place to another. In this movement there is great sacrifice. Jesus left his place of comfort to move to a foreign land. John wrote, "In the beginning was the Word, and the Word was with God, and the Word was God. . . . He came to that which was his own, but his own did not receive Him" (1:1, 11). The movement from heaven to earth was intentional. Jesus was fully immersed in a particular context and culture to call into existence a transnational community that would one day continue his ministry and carry on his mission in like fashion.

Because of Jesus' keen ability to identify with a people and his willingness to relocate from one place to another, the incarnation also shows *solidarity*. This aspect of the incarnation reveals Christ's deep concern for people in the margins. Even the Matthean genealogical account, which was meant to focus on the Word in particular, offers important cues. Jesus' way of ruling would focus on the needs of those who are often bereft of social privileges and deprived of social justice. Even when Matthew is interested in showing that Jesus is fully a man from Israel, he gives indications of God's interest in those who were often excluded. He includes names such as Tamar, Rahab, and Ruth in the genealogy, thereby revealing God's own concern for the outcast, the poor, and the immigrant.

Finally, the incarnation reveals *vulnerability*. The Son surrendered the use of his divine attributes to limit his divine power as he relied on the power of the Spirit to carry out his ministry. The act of *kenosis* (a self-emptying process) was deliberately at work in the incarnation, and Jesus depended daily on the Spirit to guide his mission. Through prayer and surrender, Jesus showed us the way to true joy and peace, as he subjected himself to the will of the Father and trusted that his obedience would lead him back to life. His vulnerability, self-emptying, and nakedness on the cross ultimately brought complete deliverance for all those who place their trust in him.

Jesus' Holistic Ministry on Earth

As Jesus became fully immersed in a particular cultural milieu, he adopted certain cultural and religious traditions of the people to which he came to save. As was his custom since childhood, Jesus would visit synagogues frequently. In fact, it was at a synagogue that he inaugurated his ministry in Nazareth when he read from the scroll: "The Spirit of the Lord is on me, because he has anointed me to preach good news to the poor. He has sent me to proclaim freedom for the prisoners, recovery of sight of the blind, to release the oppressed, and to proclaim the year of the Lord's favor" (Luke 4:18–19). All spoke well of him initially and were amazed at his gracious words (4:22) until Jesus began to speak about the inclusion of Gentiles, which included the poor and the outcasts (4:26–27). Then, the people in the synagogue were furious and drove him out of town in order to throw him off a cliff (4:28–29). Even when Jesus was despised and rejected by his own, his work had profound impact as he journeyed through the land. The kingdom of God was dawning in the ministry of Jesus to bring about his purpose of redemption and restoration for all creation.

Thomas Oden describes Jesus' work in a threefold way, even though this categorization was not formulated originally by Oden: Jesus is prophet, priest, and King.[5] These conceptualizations reflect an implicit and familiar order in the ministry of Jesus. Jesus first appeared as a prophet whom God raised up from among his own people (Acts 3:22), then as a priest in the order of Melchizedek (Heb 7:17), and finally as the King of Kings (Rev 17:14). Christ's earthly ministry begins with a prophetic role, readily seen in the way he challenged the religious officials and scribes of the day, who were more concerned with outward appearances than with the souls of humankind (Matt 23:25). His prophetic ministry is also seen through his divine healing and deliverances. The Gospels recount Jesus' confrontation with and power over evil (Mark 1:22–24; Matt 8:16; Luke 4:40–41). Jesus came to free people from the grip of the devil (1 John 3:8) as well as from adherence to a religious system that kept them in bondage. Interestingly enough, the first healing recorded in Mark is the deliverance of an individual inside the Capernaum synagogue who had an unclean spirit. Since only Jewish men were allowed in the synagogue, it is striking that Mark would describe the first miracle of Jesus as occurring in the synagogue, perhaps to defy the hypocrisy of leaders who were caught up in their own ignorance. Those who happened to be

5. Oden, *Classic Christianity,* 366.

inside the synagogue were amazed at the "new teaching" that Jesus had powerfully displayed that day (Mark 1:27).

Jesus' ministry was marked not only by power, but also by grace. The gospel narratives describe several cases where Jesus dignified the lives of outcasts because he had compassion on them (Matt 9:36). His compassion reached the masses who felt lonely and forgotten on the outskirts of society. Stories such as the woman who had been suffering for twelve years and was healed (Luke 8:43–48), a paralyzed man who was lowered through the roof and began to walk at Jesus' command (Mark 2:1–12), the man who had been an invalid for thirty-eight years and did not have anyone to help him into the healing waters (John 5:1–15), the little girl who was thought to be dead and was raised miraculously by Jesus (Mark 5:35–43), and other stories—all provide evidence of Jesus' care and grace towards the hurting.

Christ continually proclaimed the liberating news of the gospel. When Jesus sent out his twelve disciples, he gave them power and authority (Luke 9:1), commissioning them to "heal the sick, raise the dead, cleanse those who have leprosy, and drive out demons" (Matt 10:8). When Jesus sent out the seventy-two, he gave them authority to trample on snakes and scorpions and to overcome all the power of the enemy (Luke 10:19). The prophetic ministry of Jesus was carried out both through word and deed. Although Jesus was more than a prophet, he did not refute the Samaritan woman when she acknowledged him as such: "I can see that you are a prophet" (John 4:19). In fact, he himself referred to his role in this way: "Only in his hometown and in his own house is a prophet without honor" (Matt 13:57). Jesus affirmed his prophetic ministry as an important aspect of his work. His earthly ministry drew crowds and attracted the masses because the power of the Spirit was at work in him.

Christ's ministry, however, was not exclusively focused on the miraculous; it was also marked by profound depth. His teachings and daily interactions with people revealed his authority as a rabbi, a teacher of the law. His famous Sermon on the Mount became the hallmark of his teachings, unraveling the blessings that stem from holy living and setting forth guidelines to ensure this favorable outcome. His teachings were not only dialectical. Jesus also spoke through obscure parables so that their hidden meaning and mysteries would be made known only to his followers. The crowds followed him because Christ satisfied their physical needs, but his disciples followed him to learn how to live as a chosen people. Christ's teachings had deep implications for those who chose to follow him. They were to "take up their cross" and "deny themselves" (Matt 16:24). His invitation was not always well received, and many people turned away, such as a young rich ruler (Luke 18:18–23). Nevertheless, God can accomplish his purposes through a small remnant, as he is not constrained by or dependent on what the world values as important.

Finally, we find the work of Jesus as priest throughout his earthly ministry as an intercessor (Heb 5:7), mediator of grace (Heb 9:15), and sacrificial offering (Heb 5:1). The priestly role of Jesus is most clearly depicted on the cross, where he sacrificed his own life and offered it as a gift back to God who had given him as a gift to the world. Tom Noble captures this magnificent role: "This unique High Priest, *as a living, thinking, choosing human being,* obediently, but voluntarily, and as our representative, embodying all humankind in himself, offered *himself* to God."[6] On the cross, the act of ultimate love for humanity was realized.

The Centrality of the Cross

Although the identity of Jesus is broadly defined by the nature of his life, it is most visibly understood through his death and resurrection. On the cross, Jesus absorbed the full force of darkness and turned it into a movement of divine love. On the cross, Jesus embraced the full range of human sinfulness and drew it into a sphere of divine grace. On the cross, Jesus submitted to the will of the Father and, in turn, set many captives free. The cross is not

6. Noble, *Holy Trinity,* 148.

the end. On the contrary, it is the beginning of faith; it shows the extent of grace and reveals God's never-ending love for humanity.

Most scholarly discussions of the Christ event have focused on the primacy of the *theologia crucis* (the crucified Christ).[7] And rightly so, for to fail to describe the centrality of the cross would seriously mar our understanding of the purpose of Christ's mission. First, the cross has been described as "divine solidarity,"[8] "divine self-giving,"[9] and a "victory proclaimed."[10] This giving and receiving are clearly conceived as a process of interchange. In this mutual exchange, it becomes evident that through a circular movement of love, light emerges from the darkest moment in the life of the giver. But it would be wrong to look at the *theologia crucis* purely in a loving way. The cross is also an offense with a heavy weight that crushes the weak in a world where the powerful often use violence to exert their authority. We might be initially disturbed by the cruel method employed by those who killed Jesus. But it is there, where evil meets love, that we can perceive the purposes of God, which far exceed the detrimental effects of evil in the heart of humankind and in the world at large.

Historically, the cross was literally considered a death sentence. It was a form of torture that the Romans employed to punish offenders of the law. The hands and feet of criminals would be tied or nailed to a wooden beam, and they would remain hanging until they died by exhaustion or asphyxiation. The crucifixion of Jesus was even more pernicious as he was mocked, falsely accused, humiliated, and beaten along the way. His execution was not only an exclusion of his rights but an eradication of his dignity. He was made vulnerable by those in power, despised by the crowds, and deserted by his followers. And he was seemingly abandoned by his Father. Truthfully, God never left him, but in Christ's most excruciating and suffocating moment, he could not sense or recognize the Father's presence. Having taken all humanity's darkness upon

---

7. Noble, *Holy Trinity*, 158–59.

8. Moltmann, *The Spirit of Life*, 137.

9. Volf, *Exclusion and Embrace*, 13.

10. Newbigin, *Mission in Christ's Way*, 50.

himself, he became sin on the cross, with the purpose of redeeming and transforming it so that we could become the righteousness of God (2 Cor 5:21).

No doubt, the cross was used as a destructive instrument that brought humiliation and torture in the throes of death, but in Christ the cross became a powerful instrument that extends restoration in the prospects of new life. If historically the cross was man's way of dealing with sinners, figuratively the cross became God's way of redeeming sinners. The cross had been an image of subjugation and destitution; in Christ it became a symbol of liberation and forbearance. The cross of Jesus is not just a story of great endurance, sacrificial giving, and extravagant love; it is a story that invites us to embark on a similar journey—a journey of surrender and victory.

The Journey to New Life

The cross is not the end of the story, and neither is the empty tomb. The empty tomb gives evidence that Christ is the true life and that darkness cannot overcome the light (John 1:5). The resurrection of Jesus simply denotes the beginning of a new creation. It symbolizes the freedom given to his followers to participate in the future through the in-breaking of the kingdom of God in the present and the promise of full participation when the kingdom of God is finally consummated. Without the resurrection, the cross would be a hopeless dead end. But because of the resurrection, the road toward salvation is possible through the empowerment of the life-giving Spirit. If the cross is a tunnel of shadows, the resurrection is a gateway to light. The resurrection is the dawn of a new morning, the bloom of new life, and the hope of more yet to come.

Because the Spirit's mission is to bring about the redemptive purposes of God in all creation, the Spirit moves in the heart of people to bring them into a community of believers to covenant and fellowship with God. The economy of our redemption is effected through the work of the Spirit, who goes ahead to prepare the way for the Word of God to be fruitful in the hearts of humanity. An indispensable grace, commonly referred to as prevenient grace, operates before we are able to respond to the saving act of God. This dispensation of God's grace is made possible through the Spirit who then offers us saving grace and healing grace.

Brazilian missiologist Valdir Steuernagel describes the way in which the Spirit of God is calling the church to collaborate with God's salvific plans with the following words: "Mission is first to perceive the blowing of the Spirit and the direction from which it comes, and then to run in the same direction to which the Spirit is blowing."[11] The church has been given a wonderful opportunity to embrace its true calling, both as a recipient of the grace of God and as an extender of the same grace to others. The Spirit is always moving, always blowing, beckoning us to become witnesses of Jesus who is the true "faithful witness" (Rev 1:5). As the church follows the Lord who redeemed it and learns to respond to his grace, the church will fulfill the purpose for which it was called into existence.

11. Quoted in Escobar, *New Global Mission*, 127.

2

A Missionary Church

THE CHURCH IS THE carrier of the good news of Jesus Christ and called to share the gospel to all peoples and all generations. As the social and cultural contexts of our world keep changing, the gospel needs a fresh telling to make it applicable in the contemporary world. Life is a journey of discovery where our views of the other must be continually examined. Negatively, this means that the church will have to own its failure for focusing on internal preferences rather than on the purpose for which it exists—transformation of lives and society. Positively, this awareness might help the church shift and refocus its priorities to minister in meaningful and creative ways in the times in which it lives.

The present age is the age of the Spirit, who applies the redemptive work of the Son to the lives of individuals by calling them, indwelling them, and sending them out into the world as vehicles of grace. The church, as a reflection and carrier of Christ's mission, is the aroma of Christ. However, the church's agenda has not always been aligned with the purposes of Christ. At times, the church has been overly concerned with quantifiable metrics and infrastructure developments, sacrificing the command "to go" to the nations on the altar of staying comfortably "at home." But the calling to take the gospel around the world has not ceased, and it beckons us to consider anew what it means to carry the church forward in such a time as this.

The past twenty years have been saturated with many different forms of ministries and strategies seeking to revitalize the church and make it relevant to society, from the church growth movement to the emergent church to the missional church discussion. We have also engaged in practical conversations that affirm the deep crisis the church is experiencing in terms of its feeble spirituality seeking to propose a way forward. Meanwhile, entire groups of people around the world remain unevangelized, while others have walked away and remain adrift because of the church's perceived irrelevance to daily life. If the church is at the very center of God's purposes in the world and is the sign and foretaste of his Kingdom, then world evangelization requires the "whole Church to take the whole gospel to the whole world."[1] This is a daunting task, one that requires ongoing cultural analysis, theological reflection, contextual application, and ecumenical collaboration.

A Divine Gift to the World

The church is truly a gift, even when it might not always be perceived or received as such. The church has been traditionally depicted in different ways to understand its influence and role in the world: as an institution, sacrament, herald, servant, mystical communion, and fellowship.[2] All these descriptors hold some validity as linguistic designations of the structural arrangement, witness, and function of the church. Nevertheless, the most important constituent of the church's being and understanding should not be derived from external designations, but rather through internal ontology. This ontological reality focuses on the nature of the Spirit who gave birth to the church, made possible by the Christ event. Avery Dulles eloquently describes the church as a "divine

1. Lausanne, "Lausanne Covenant," par. 6.
2. See Dulles, *Models of the Church*.

self-gift"[3] in which God's new creation through the church becomes the very dwelling place of the triune God. It is in the life of its gathered and scattered people that the Spirit manifests his presence through the sacramental and communal life of his people. An adequate framework for understanding the role of the church, then, is located within God's own eschatological work. This understanding invites the church to see itself not as a self-originating institution, but rather as a continuation of God's purposeful means to make himself known through a people.

In some ways, the church may be considered a mystery, although not exclusively. It is not a mystery in the sense of unintelligibility or enigmatic subjectivity, but in that it relates and narrates the richness of its inheritance. The church is not only a mystery, but also an event in the grand narrative of God's sovereign plan of salvation. On the day of Pentecost, the Spirit breathed life preemptively and redemptively into a group of praying believers. As the Spirit breathed on the disciples, he empowered them to go out, not in their own strength, but through his ever-present work in and through their lives (John 20:21–22; Acts 1:8). This epic moment rooted the church on the premise and promise that the Spirit would carry it into full maturity and use it as a vehicle of grace in the extension of God's Kingdom and Christ's reign on earth. Thus, the church is also an instrument, called to carry out the mission of Christ by way of expressing and proclaiming the liberating news of the reign of God.[4] As such, it is a vehicle and sign of the coming Kingdom and, therefore, embodies the living presence of the Spirit who moves, has his being, and is ever-so-present in the community of faith.

If the church is an instrument that serves the purposes of the coming Kingdom and is the continuation of the Christ event in history through the power of the Spirit, then Christ must remain the vision of the church. Jurgen Moltmann affirms, "The church's first word is not 'church' but Christ. The church's final word is not 'church' but the glory of the Father and the Son in the Spirit of

---

3. Dulles, *Models of the Church*, 9.

4. Newbigin, *The Open Secret*, 40–42

liberty."[5] Moltmann believes that Christology should be treated as the dominant theme in ecclesiology. Nevertheless, the foundation for understanding the doctrine of the church relies not simply or specifically on Christological conceptions, but primarily on the doctrine of God.[6] Who God is must shape the understanding of who the people of God are becoming. Therefore, how we describe the ineffable and transcendent reality of the triune God may also help to illumine how we understand the nature, purpose, and mission of the church.

The Relational Nature of God

The unity of the Trinity can help the church understand its cohesion and distinctives. The Trinity has been described as a "dance" in which the interdependent, mutually internal, and reciprocal giving and receiving are made possible by virtue of an ongoing interpenetration of each person without losing or dissolving their personal distinctiveness.[7] This internal mutuality, known as *perichoresis* in Greek, is a "coming and going," where the Trinity is said to live in "circulatory movement,"[8] resembling a "community of being,"[9] and acting as a "society of persons united by a common divinity."[10] Theologian Clark Pinnock writes, "Social Trinity means that there are three persons who are subjects in the divine experiences."[11] At the very core, one must conclude, the nature of God is utterly relational.

In creation, we find all Persons of the Trinity present, involved, and participating, but the Father is clearly the one creating.

5. Moltmann, *The Church in the Power of the Spirit*, 6.

6. Several scholars have articulated this view because the nature of God informs the nature of the people of God. Among these scholars are Miroslav Volf and Terry Cross.

7. Volf, *After Our Likeness*, 209.

8. Cross, *The People of God's Presence*, 50.

9. McGrath, *Christian Theology*, 306.

10. Pinnock, *Flame of Love*, 35.

11. Pinnock, *Flame of Love*, 35.

Similarly, the entire Trinity is immersed in the work of redemption, but this is often interpreted as the distinctive activity of the Son. Likewise, the Trinity fosters a sense of community among those called, but it is the Spirit who enlivens what is dead, serving as the "bond of love"[12] that unites the Father and the Son in perfect harmony. But the Spirit is also present in the cosmos, hovering over the created order, drawing all people to himself, and thereby bonding and drawing others to the Godhead.

The doctrine of God, then, reveals the essential unity embedded in the plurality of its social entity. Certainly, God displays several attributes that portray his nature. He is holy, perfect in love, good, gracious, kind, and omnipotent. Therefore, God cannot contradict his nature in his external workings. Although we cannot fully reflect the nature of God in this world, we are being transformed into his likeness daily. The optimism of the gospel and the radical transformative power of God permeate the inner fabric of the church calling it to embrace its identity more fully in the journey toward wholeness and reconciliation. The essence of the church, therefore, reflects the relationality that exists within the Trinity itself. But such relational endeavor must be built on the foundations already laid by the early conciliar decrees of the church, where there was unity about what the Scriptures taught. John Wesley reminds us of the importance of a commitment to ancient orthodoxy: "But whatever doctrine is *new* must be wrong; for the *old* religion is the only *true one;* and no doctrine can be right, unless it is the very same 'which was from the beginning.'"[13]

The Nature of the Church

If the nature of God is relational at its core, being one in essence and three in persons, might this concept shed light on how we ought to understand the church? In seeking to clarify how the inner-trinitarian life may be helpful in understanding the nature of

12. Pinnock, *Flame of Love,* 40.

13. Wesley, *On Sin in Believers,* Part I, par. 9.

the church, Terry Cross affirms the equality and value of each person while recognizing that each member of the body also differs in functionality or practical operation. Cross states, "God's own manner of assessing humans is initially based on who they are rather than what they do; this must be the starting point for all of our interactions both inside and outside the Christian Community."[14] He also contends that "while humans may put a high value on *functions*, God places a higher value on *essence*."[15] This analysis is helpful in explaining why the community of faith has often fallen prey to its own preoccupations with activities and programs at the expense of pursuing its highest virtues. Nevertheless, such perspective fails to recognize that function and essence do not have to be separated but can be fully integrated, as one flows out of the other and the two are inextricably related.

Because the various gifts, callings, and ministries of the Christian community correspond to the divine plurality clearly expressed in the activities of the different Persons of the Trinity, the function of the church is not only specific but also universal in purpose and eternal in dimension. That is, the church's specific purpose is *doxological* (to bring glory to God), its universal purpose is *prototypical* (to represent the new creation), and its ethereal dimension is *proleptic* (to be a kingdom of priests in the present, foreshadowing its role in eternity).

The priestly prayer of Jesus that invites those who believe in him to share the relational unity of the triune God describes these functions very well. The unity that Jesus calls the new creation to embrace does not mean *uniformity*. This would be impossible because the people of God come from different traditions, cultural backgrounds, and lifestyles. Consequently, as cultural beings we have all acquired unique habits shaped by the time period in which we live, the generational cohort to which we belong, the cultural influences that have shaped us, and so on. The unity Christ calls us to is *doxological*: "Glory has come to me through them" (Jn 17:10).

14. Cross, *The People of God's Presence*, 58.

15. Cross, *The People of God's Presence*, 58.

The unity Christ prays for his body to experience is also *prototypical* in that Christ sets us apart to be sent out as his representatives in the world: "As you sent me in to the world, I have sent them into the world" (John 17:18) and "I pray also for those who will believe in me through their message" (John 17:20b). The unity that Christ desires is one of heart—so that the Father may be glorified through his body. This unity is attainable only when we lay down our lives and personal preferences for the sake of a higher purpose—namely, to extend God's grace to the ends of the earth. Every person, as a bearer of the marks of Christ, is then duly equipped to perform their individual tasks in a manner that contributes to the advancement of the Kingdom by virtue of their calling and giftings.

Finally, the unity Christ prays for foreshadows and depicts the union we will enjoy one day at the coming glory, where we will serve as a kingdom and priests (Rev 1:6, 5:10), continuing the designation of Israel as a kingdom of priests (Exod19:6), which was also applied to the early church (1 Pet 2:5, 9). We see the continuation of the Kingdom language *proleptically* embodied in the priesthood of believers for we will serve the King for all of eternity. Jesus himself desires such involvement—"I want those you have given me to be with me where I am" (John 17:24b).

Just as the Father sent the Son, the Son sends the church through the power of his Spirit (John 20:21). The relationality inherent in the reality of the trinitarian Godhead is not confined to their circle of enjoyment. Rather, this relationality is expressed through their continual self-giving, other-loving, self-emptying and other-sending efforts, so that we may reflect and resemble the same relational unity.

Because the body of Christ is dispersed throughout hundreds of cultures, no church in a given culture can isolate itself from other churches in other cultures and no single church can claim to be sufficient in and of itself. The local church, indubitably, is a part of the universal church. As Miroslav Volf says, "We often think of a local church as a part of the universal church. We would do well also to invert the claim. Every local church is a catholic community because, in a profound sense, all other churches are a part of that church, all of them shape—or ought to shape—its identity."[16] The identity of the church is not culturally based. Neither should the church withdraw from its surrounding culture, even though at times it resorts to such a detrimental escape. The church's identity is biblically formed, underscoring its peculiar role in society as a transformer of its social location and representative of the many peoples that conform it. The identity of the church is partly shaped by the images of the church presented in the New Testament, but it is mostly established by virtue of its connection to the head of the church—Christ. After all, it is Christ who leads, guides, directs, redirects, and continually restores his broken body to also redeem and restore a broken world.

Images of the Church

God created humanity for covenantal relationship. God reveals his character and nature most fully in Christ, who inaugurated a new race. Paul uses the phrase "in Christ" to express the idea of union, but this union is not one of *essence* as much as of *purpose*: "So, if anyone is in Christ, the new creation has come" (2 Cor 5:17a); "For you are all one in Christ Jesus" (Gal 3:28); "There is now no condemnation for those who are in Christ Jesus" (Rom 8:1). Being in Christ means that the church should not only stand on the foundational truths associated with its connection to the vine as branches (John 15:1–17), but should remember the privilege the church has as Christ's heirs of a much richer and fruitful inheritance.

The imagery denoted by the designation as "body of Christ" shows the preeminence of oneness that creates a mutual bond between Christ and the church. The body should never be confused with Christ himself, but it should never be separated from Christ either. The identification of Christ is so closely linked to the body that what is done to Christ's people is done to him (Matt 25:35–45). To persecute the church is to persecute him (Acts 9:4–5). To

---

16. Volf, *Exclusion and Embrace*, 43.

sin against his people is to sin against him (1 Cor 8:12). So close is the identification between Christ and his body, the church, that the grace given to the church becomes the seed of glory that reflects the image of Christ to the world.

The bond created between Christ and the church is often understood through other images as well, such as a communion of faith, fellowship of the Spirit, and the bride of Christ. These images convey the idea that the primary factor binding the members of the church to each other is the reconciling grace of Christ, expressed through the movement of the Spirit. Harper and Metzger affirm, "Outside the Trinity, there is no Church; inside the Triune God's Church, there is salvation."[17] This view is attributed historically to Cyprian of Carthage, who suggested that apart from the church one could not be saved, because "You cannot have God for your Father if you do not have the Church for your mother."[18] The church is not Christ, but rather his representation on earth. The church, then, is our "mother" in the sense that it begets our ministry and nourishes our identity as children of God, making us heir of his redeeming grace. Volf describes the church as a daughter of faith as well as a mother of faith.[19] This dynamic relationship positions the church both as a recipient and benefactor of God's grace.

The image of motherhood assigned to the church, however, is limited and could be misleading as it seems to automatically imply birthing rather than nurturing. As Terry Cross states, "To say the church is our mother and to state there is no salvation outside of the church is to lessen the role of the Holy Spirit in the operation of salvation."[20] The church carries on the reconciling work of Christ as carrier of his grace here on earth. To say that salvation comes solely through the church's witness, ministry, and preaching, therefore, would minimize the causative power of the Spirit. God is not constrained to the inner workings of a particular group but moves to draw all people to himself in a variety of ways.

17. Harper and Metzger, *Exploring Ecclesiology*, 29.

18. Cyprian of Carthage, "The Unity of the Catholic Church," 435.

19. Volf, *After Our Likeness*, 162.

20. Cross, *The People of God's Presence*, 31.

God creates a bride for his Son, and although the New Testament does not delve into a full description of the church as the "bride of Christ," the idea that Christ loves and cares for the church in order to purify it, cleanse it, and make it holy is seen in Ephesians 5:22–27. Paul describes the death and resurrection of Christ as a necessary act in salvation history to present to himself "a radiant church, without stain or wrinkle or any other blemish, but holy and blameless" (Eph 5:27). Although this imagery could lead to a romanticized description or idealized notion, it is helpful in highlighting other aspects of the church's role and function as it prepares for union with the Godhead, indicating the importance of allegiance and necessity of purity. As the bride of Christ, the church is being prepared and refined, sharing in the righteousness and virtues of Christ. The church exists, then, to love Christ and serve his interests on earth. Bearing his name and sharing in Christ's righteousness become the path that allows the church to embrace a more gracious and faithful approach in its ministry towards others.

The Profound Mystery of the Church

As mentioned above, the Trinity as a relational, social, and perfect entity is dynamic, organic, and never changing. The church, on the other hand, is dynamic, organized, and ever-growing. The church is continually being transformed through a relational union with the Godhead. The inner workings of Christ in the church are "a profound mystery" (Eph 5:32). Yet, the church should not only be perceived as a mystical union with Christ; it is also a fellowship of the Spirit, a communion of saints, and a priesthood of believers. As such, the church must be willing to come together, remain together, rejoice together, mourn together, and pray together in response to the calling of God. The Spirit who formed the first ecclesial community continues to gather and scatter God's people to participate in his "self-giving and other-receiving love."[21] It is

---

21. Volf, *Exclusion and Embrace*, 127.

the Spirit who sustains the church, calling it to embody and journey together through a meaningful partnership as it becomes a co-participant in God's restorative work in the created order.

The church as a fellowship and communion invites others to belong, find a place to share their gifts, and be affirmed and valued as human beings. This image shifts our view of the church as a social in-group to that of an out-group that makes room for the other. This participation in the life of the Spirit can be complete, however, only as the church aims its efforts toward three fronts: *upward*, as it fellowships with the Spirit; *inward*, as it grows in the faith; and *outward*, as it welcomes strangers and the least of these. The Spirit himself turns our fear of the other into an opportunity to embrace the other. Because fear is the destroyer of hope and hope is the engine of life, the church must first be willing to face and defeat its own fears. As Cross reflects, "If God opens Godself up to being wounded, how can God's people expect to operate within the walls of a sanctuary in safety?"[22] The community of faith must operate as a haven for the weary, a refuge for the weak, and a clinic for the wounded. In such circumstances, the church becomes ripe for a fresh encounter with the Spirit who comes at every turn to address the church's anemic condition and broken state, turning its condition around and setting it ablaze through the power of the living God.

The Church and Its Mission

Ecclesiology has been built on the pillars of doctrinal and creedal understandings, as explained in the previous sections. Missiology, on the other hand, is primarily concerned with how the church embodies those doctrines and activates them through faithful application in service to the world. Because God's mission preceded the formation of the church, the church carries on the work initiated by God. Andrew Kirk affirms: "The Church is by nature missionary to the extent that, if it ceases to be missionary, it has not only failed in

22. Cross, *The People of God's Presence*, 85.

one of its tasks, it has ceased to be the Church."[23] At the core, then, the church is the transporter of all missionary endeavors around the globe, enabled by a missionary God.

As a visible sign of the presence of Christ and carrier of the gospel message, the church has a mandate to go into the whole world and share the good news. If God calls his church to bear witness to the in-breaking of his Kingdom, how can those who have witnessed the new reality of God's transforming grace partner with God in this task? When it comes to the manner in which the church is to engage in this journey, missiologists have often disagreed. Whereas some have emphasized proclaiming the gospel as a necessary means by which to share God's purposes on earth, others have affirmed that the world's social and economic needs should dictate the agenda. These views have often arisen from a truncated understanding of the role and tasks of mission.

Missions, in the words of John Stott, "is not a word for everything the church does . . . [but] describes rather everything the church is sent into the world to do."[24] That is, just as Christ sends his church into the world as his Father has sent him, so the church is called to permeate the fabric of society with the good news of salvation. Although this salvation begins with the promise of redemption and restoration, it is not limited to the spiritual dimension. It must also show concern for the physical aspects of life, bringing justice and reconciliation to the broken systems and social relationships all around us.

The church is not meant to be an exclusionary group of people who enjoy God's saving grace within the confinement of their own benefit. They are the means by which God intends to save the many. As Michael Goheen says, "The elect community *makes known* God's universal purpose as a reconciled people, and the elect community *brings about* God's universal purpose as a reconciling people."[25] It is ultimately the social and cosmic nature of salvation that brings about God's purposes on earth. The Greek

23. Kirk, *What is Mission*, 31.

24. Stott, *Christian Mission*, 48.

25. Goheen, *The Church and Its Vocation*, 32.

word *sōtēria*, most often translated as "salvation," has a wide array of possible interpretations: rescue, deliverance, preservation, restoration, and healing.[26] Thus, salvation is "the good news of God's reign of peace, justice, and freedom for all, especially the poor, oppressed, and marginalized around the world."[27] The good news of the gospel impacts all spheres of life and is expressed as a past, present, and future reality.

The mission of God ultimately belongs to God, but he desires to accomplish it through a group of people who serve as his representatives on earth. Paul Hiebert describes this interdependent relationship between the story of God and the story of humanity in the simplest of ways: "The history of humankind is first and foremost the story of God's mission to redeem sinners who seek salvation, the story of Jesus who came as a missionary, and the story of God's Spirit who works in the hearts of those who hear."[28] Our story is inseparable from the story of God. And just as God's story is one of sending and discipling, the church mirrors God's story as it sends out disciples to make disciples of all the nations.

Confronting Western Individualism

The church is the means by which the kingdom of God can be visibly manifested in the world because Christ is in the church. The whole body of Christ has been entrusted to steward the mystery of Christ and to make the "hope of glory" known among the nations (Col 1:27–28). There can be no personal growth apart from the body of Christ because "the body is not made up of one part but of many," and we can only exert our function as a part of the body within the body itself (1 Cor 12:14).

A leading factor behind the barrenness that is so prevalent in the Christian landscape of the Western church is the value of individualism inherent in Western culture, which stands in

26. Oden, *Classic Christianity*, 562.

27. Tizon, *Whole and Reconciled*, 74.

28. Hiebert, *Anthropological Insights*, 17.

diametrical opposition to the value of community so evident in the Scriptures—a value clearly displayed in other cultures around the world. Some researchers have suggested that individualism serves as a survival mechanism, teaching the value of individual responsibility, which is a necessary component in the healthy formation of personhood.[29] But the individualism prevalent in Western culture has influenced and shaped the Western church to the point of diluting and undermining the essence of the Christian faith. This has led the church into a deficient state characterized by a fascination with numbers and infrastructure.

Western individualism has placed the self at the center of the universe. From an extravagant focus on self-care to the lyrics of contemporary pop music, we find that the self is valued above anything or anyone else. For instance, American singer Bebe Rexha penned a song titled "Call on Me" in which she vividly, and perhaps unknowingly, expresses the type of narcissism that often lurks underneath the surface of individualism:

> If I need a lover, someone to hold me
> Satisfy all my needs
> If I need a lover, someone to save me
> Someone to set me free
> I'd call on me
> I'd call on me.

This kind of self-reliance, excessive love for oneself, and unbounded admiration of self has permeated the social fabric of Western culture.

Christianity stands as a corrective to this cultural trend, where the church is dependent on the grace of God and must be interdependent. The evangelical tradition has stressed the need to make a personal decision for Christ. To say that the journey of faith requires personal commitment is a tautology because salvation is *individual*. But salvation is far from being *individualized* or *individualistic*. Salvation is social; it is all-encompassing and carries deep implications for our social relationships and reconciliation

---

29. Plueddemann, *Leading Across Cultures*, 115.

with each other. But the heavy emphasis on simply getting people saved instead of focusing on creating reconciled communities has led the church to a fragile and feeble state. The church has turned inward, offering a cheap grace that can be attained through a simple prayer, regarding salvation as a transactional endeavor. As a result, the church tries to beautify a ship that keeps sinking in the midst of a rapidly changing culture that seems hesitant at best to enter the ship. The liberal tradition, on the other hand, has helped set our vision toward the restoration of society with its emphasis on social justice, liberation, and freedom from oppressive systems. These critical elements, which echo Christ's own missional concerns, have influenced the church in positive ways. Yet, even with this direction taken, what has been often overlooked is the importance of living a sacramental life within the community of faith. That is, our individual goals must be surrendered to the plans of the crucified Lord with the hope that the soul will be liberated by the Spirit rather than by its own efforts. In that way, the community will grow together and mature as disciples of Christ who make disciples around the nations.

One way to fight the forces of individualism is to participate in multicultural churches, where communal life and worship are expressed in the context of cross-cultural communities who highly value collectivism—a societal value that prioritizes the group over individual goals. Here, individualism can be challenged as the church gathers together as the fellowship of believers across racial and ethnic lines. God forms the visible gathering of his people to bring us along in his mission of reconciliation. The church is not only the visible gathering of believers here on earth, but also the new society in the present age that has already tasted the powers of the age to come. Not only has the church been blessed with the great promise that the Holy Spirit would be poured out upon all men and women, but it has also been called to anticipate on earth the life of heaven. Therefore, the church lives out this eschatological reality as it is guided by the Spirit in diverse and transcultural contexts. The promise that one day every language, tribe, and nation will worship at the foot of the King can help us understand why it is necessary to start putting that reality into practice here on earth.

Missional Discipleship

The Western church has been increasingly concerned with activities, offering attractive programs to retain its members, building appealing structures and services to attract new members, and participating in benevolent pursuits. In recent decades, however, the understanding of the church's mission has begun to shift. This transformation has ensued partly as a result of cultural and social changes affecting the religious landscape of the nation warning us to stop looking inward. It has also stemmed from new perspectives promoted by the "missional church" discussion, which has urged the church to focus on the mission of God as the overarching narrative that guides the mission of the church.[30]

While the understanding of the role of the church as centered on the purposes of God has taken root in various academic circles, often missing from its application is clear and practical reflection on disciple making as the primary goal of the church's mission. In a thought-provoking article entitled "Why the Missional Movement Will Fail," Mike Breen surprised many of his readers with poignant remarks regarding the missional movement, comparing the missional church to a new car with no engine. He proposed that the engine of the church is discipleship, and that without a proper understanding and implementation of its significance to the Christian faith, the church will remain stagnant, unable to move forward. Several other voices have joined Breen in his concern to show that the cornerstone and the pathway to success for the missional church movement lie in rediscovering its missing link, namely "missional discipleship."[31]

---

30. For a thorough discussion of the missional church movement, see Guder, *Missional Church: A Vision for the Sending of the Church in North America.*

31. See Beard, "Missional Discipleship."

As can be observed, the primary commission for the church, as given by Jesus himself, is not only one of proclamation and social justice but of disciple making. True discipleship takes place when we move beyond conveying information to heart transformation. Disciple making is the evidence of a robust spirituality, as it seeks to nurture other individuals in the environment of the Christian community for the greater works of the Kingdom.

Unfortunately, the church has not always maintained a balanced perspective concerning what disciple making entails. At times, the church has overly emphasized the place of individual practices at the expense of other equally important elements, such as living life in community or engaging in social justice efforts. This tendency, which Halter and Smay call "a lopsided process," is far too common.[32] At other times, the church has failed to engage in any formation process at all or has been unable to provide the means by which disciples can overcome their sinful and selfish tendencies. As Halter and Smay poignantly note, these barriers "represent the fight of the Spirit to win out over the flesh and the battle against a globally satanic, organized, and intentional world system that traps our people, making them one-sided, no-sided, or dead spiritually."[33] Thus, Halter and Smay suggest that a missional disciple must keep several elements in balance: communion, mission, and community. Missional discipleship involves maintaining an invigorating relationship with the triune God, forming a deep sense of belonging among fellow disciples, and displaying an intentional life of service to our surrounding culture. This can be possible only when we allow Jesus to help us step forward into his eternal purposes one day at a time.

Missional Tasks and Holistic Ministry

Many are the tasks, duties, and privileges of the church. Craig Ott and Stephen Strauss understand the church's responsibilities in

32. Halter and Smay, *Gathered and Scattered Church*, 98.

33. Halter and Smay, *Gathered and Scattered Church*, 100.

the world in terms of two mandates: the creation mandate and the gospel mandate. They trace this classification back to the work of the Reformers who claimed that there were two main aspects in redemption: personal transformation and God's providential grace in creation.[34] This dual focus has been reflected in a tendency to evaluate the church's mission priorities as falling into two parallel categories—evangelism and social action. Throughout the years, these two emphases have often been treated as polar opposites, leading to endless debates on how the tasks of the church should be oriented and prioritized. More recently, with the rise of the philosophy of integral mission, this discussion has no longer been a point of contention. On the contrary, the emphasis has shifted to balance and integration, as both priorities carry weight for effective missional endeavors.

Both mandates are necessary for the fulfillment of Christ's Great Commission and Great Commandment. The creation mandate seeks to maintain a just society, focusing on the stewardship of creation and the reordering of structures and organizations to make them more equitable and just. The gospel mandate, on the other hand, is concerned with the proclamation of the message of Christ through evangelism, discipleship, and church planting. Ott and Strauss, like the proponents of integral mission, see an interdependent relationship between the two. They affirm that "fulfilling the gospel mandate leads to deep-level fulfillment of the creation mandate as a source of God's love and values," and conversely that "fulfilling the creation mandate leads to credible fulfillment of the gospel mandate as expression of God's love."[35] This interdependent and symbiotic relationship provides a complementary understanding of the calling and work of the church. Nevertheless, some missiologists still position the gospel mandate as holding a fundamental role in the fulfillment of the Great Commission, as only through reconciliation with God can the creation mandate be properly fulfilled. They affirm that it is in relationship with God that the church can move beyond salvation to impact the social

34. Ott et al., *Encountering Theology of Missions*, 149.

35. Ott et al., *Encountering Theology of Missions*, 154.

order.[36] Because the gospel mandate is more specific to the church than the creation mandate, it is not unreasonable to consider the gospel mandate the church's leading concern.

However, neither the creation mandate nor the gospel mandate should be framed or understood as anthropocentric callings in which the agents of mission are the people. Although framing the responsibility of the church in this way may seem like a comprehensive way to express God's concern for the well-being of humanity, providing a clearer understanding of what the gospel mandate entails is necessary. The gospel mandate must be centered on the Christ that the church preaches. As members of a new humanity, the church is instructed to bring renewal and transformation to the social order in all its dimensions. But this calling can never be adequately fulfilled unless the presence of Christ through the Spirit empowers the community of faith. Keeping in mind that the tasks or activities of the church can never be divorced from its doxological purpose as a community will better position the church to develop a robust engagement with God's plans for the redemption and restoration of all things.

The activities of the church may vary as they stem from the various callings and giftedness of its members. Some individuals may be more naturally inclined or spiritually equipped to engage in the gospel mandate through preaching, church planting, discipleship, spiritual formation practices, or healing and deliverance ministries. Others may be more inclined to work in the public square or focus on ecological issues, humanitarian efforts, political or social liberation, thus fulfilling the creation mandate more specifically. Because the church is the only society that exists for the sake of the world, the church must become more intentional in its efforts to attend to the realities of the contemporary world.

The tasks that the church carries out in its desire to collaborate with God's project for the world make the church a missionary church. Bearing witness to the gospel through proclamation and becoming agents of reconciliation form the backbone of missions. As John Stott reminds us, loving our neighbor does not refer only

36. Ott et al., *Encountering Theology of Missions*, 155.

to a "bodiless soul that we should love only his soul, nor a soulless body that we should care for its welfare alone."[37] The gospel reveals the twofold nature of Christ's all-encompassing mission, as he came both to rescue the lost (Luke 19:10) and to set the captives free (Luke 4:18–21). It is *his* mission of rescue. Our part is to simply give witness to the freedom and joy that we have found because he first found us.

Beyond Tasks and Beyond Us

As times change, the mission of the church needs constant renewal and reconceptualization. How do we convey the gospel message in a way that is relevant to contemporary life without dissolving or diluting its essential purpose? How do we make room for God to move in fresh ways? Several scholars have proposed to move beyond the dualism of the "word and deed" paradigm to include a third component—signs. This proposal was largely framed by Charismatics and Pentecostals who emphasize the creative power of the Spirit. They contend that evangelism and social action, while clearly important, should not be separated from the supernatural activity and active presence of the Spirit in the community of faith.[38] Al Tizon indicates that missiologists have used different terminologies to describe a mission that is holistic and God-centered. Among the words selected to describe such a relationship are "whole," "transformational," "power evangelism," "integral," and "signs and wonders." Tizon contends that these interests arise from a deep concern "to convey the width and breadth of the gospel, and therefore the width and breadth of the church's mission."[39]

Although these voices coming from within Pentecostalism articulate the importance of including the signs and wonders of the Spirit who moves beyond our understanding, it would be imprudent to normalize such signs as one of the central tasks of

37. Stott, *Christian Mission*, 47.

38. Tizon, *Whole and Reconciled*, 163.

39. Tizon, *Whole and Reconciled*, 164.

the mission of the church. Certainly, this innovative addition provides an important corrective to the traditional understanding of the workings of God through the church. The Holy Spirit gives supernatural gifts to advance his Kingdom in ways we may not always desire nor feel comfortable expressing. Nevertheless, many well-documented cases confirm God's supernatural movement in the modern world and give evidence of the power of the Spirit to further the mission of God in this way.[40] Although there is validity in considering this third component a possible means by which the mission of the church can advance, signs and wonders should be viewed as God's mysterious workings and not a normative expectation that the church should embrace in its missional tasks. Because God moves outside of our understanding, we should not limit the ways in which he may choose to use the church to expand his Kingdom. But because God moves through reasonable approaches, we should also be cautious of undue emphasis on his supernatural activity in the world.

A few remarks are necessary to summarize this discussion. First, most Westerners are not accustomed to the idea that God moves miraculously, preferring a more naturalistic approach to understanding events that do not seem to have a rational explanation. Westerners often perceive "miracles" to be something that science has not yet explained or something that we don't yet have the ability to understand. On the other hand, individuals from the Majority World have been more aware of such occurrences because supernatural manifestations are more prevalent and their worldview allows for such understandings to explain causation. Involvement in witchcraft, occult practices, or satanic rituals has driven many people in the Majority World to seek the power of God to break such curses, and thus to pursue the power-driven gifts of the Spirit to overcome their effects. Naturalistic worldviews that do not allow or account for these types of realities and dismiss them as superstition will simply attribute these effects to natural

40. See Keener, *Miracles Today* for a critical evaluation of this topic, including research-based case studies.

reasons, such as mental conditions, dismissing root causes which may be spiritual in nature.

Second, simply because one may not be familiar with these types of ministry or remain highly suspicious, this does not mean that individuals who are gifted in this kind of ministry should not use signs and wonders as a means of effective missional engagement. When new ideas emerge or situations call for different approaches, we should always seek to understand, evaluate, discern, confirm, test, and take time to perform good research so that we arrive at well-informed conclusions.

Finally, just as theological training is of utmost importance to develop sound leaders, so is adequate training in healing-focused ministries. While evangelism and social action should remain the church's top priorities, mission should not be limited to these two categories as they are generally understood. God moves outside of our realm of understanding to reveal himself; therefore, we should not be reluctant to follow his movement. Because the primary role of a miracle or wonder is to authenticate biblical revelation in fresh missional settings, remaining open to God's supernatural activity will bring glory to him and will help the church advance in new and fresh ways.

Part II

Navigating New Patterns

3

Interactivity in the Digital Age

As THE PREVIOUS CHAPTER described, in recent decades Christians have turned to a more robust and comprehensive understanding of missions by accepting the social as well as the evangelistic responsibility of the gospel. God sent his Son on a mission to transform the world, heal broken relationships, and redeem humanity from their sin. In the contemporary world, people interact daily with others and yet seem to be worlds apart. Economic, environmental, humanitarian, and ecological crises have reconfigured the world. How do we embrace the gospel in the midst of these dramatic socio-cultural shifts and share it in meaningful ways?

Amidst all these crises, the technological revolution of our digital era has created opportunities for unprecedented types of social engagement and relational connections. Innovative interactions formed around virtual communities may at times be superficial, but they can certainly become tools for powerful witness. Before describing the opportunities and challenges of ministry through the virtual world, I will discuss ways in which social interactions have been changing due to technological advances. The theory of social capital provides a framework by which to understand and take advantage of the opportunities offered by virtual platforms and to a brief history of the theory I now turn.

The Progression of Social Capital

Although the concept has seen an extensive range of definitions, social capital can be largely understood as the social ties formed between individuals and groups. These ties make it possible for resources to be shared, information to flow, and cooperation to develop, so as to facilitate action in society and generate potential personal and communal benefits. The theory was originally formulated by sociologists and has been adopted in the fields of economics and political science while inspiring research in medicine, business, criminology, social psychology, mass communication, religious studies, and other fields. For example, the concept of social capital has been used to illumine issues such as economic development, rural and urban development, community development, career success, access to employment opportunities, the value of education, civic involvement, immigration, religion, corruption, and the shift of social involvement to nontraditional platforms such as cyberspace and the virtual community.[1]

In its early phases of research, social capital was viewed as a set of features in a social structure that could lead to collective action in order to bring about mutual benefit for the community. Decades later, attention shifted to gains and benefits for the individual. One of the voices who made practical applications of the concept was Mark Granovetter. By distinguishing between "strong ties" (family and intimate friends) and "weak ties" (acquaintances),

---

1. On economic development, Putnam, *Making Democracy Work* and Woolcock and Narayan, "Social Capital: Implications for Development Theory, Research, and Policy"; on rural development, Hanifan, "Appalachia: The Rural School Community Center" and Jacobs, *The Death and Life of Great American Cities*"; on community development, Gittel and Vidal, *Community Organizing: Building Social Capital as a Development Strategy*; on career success, Burt, *Structural Holes*; on employment opportunities, Granovetter, "Strength of Weak Ties"; on education, Coleman, *Social Capital in the Creation of Human Capital*; on civic involvement, Putnam, *Bowling Alone*; on immigration, Portes, "The Two Meanings of Social Capital;" on religion, Wuthnow, "Religious Involvement and Status-Bridging Social Capital;" on corruption, Graeff, "Social Capital: The Dark Side"; on cyberspace and virtual communities, Lin, *Social Capital* and Littau, "The Virtual Social Capital of Online Communities."

Granovetter argued that weak ties would enable a person to advance professionally, leading to "better access to job information."[2]

This early perspective would be challenged by French sociologist Pierre Bourdieu, who described social capital in terms of resources, group membership, and networks.[3] Despite Bourdieu's strides to highlight the important role of social capital in terms of the resource exchanges it can enact, his work would be slightly overshadowed by that of a contemporary theoretician, James Coleman. Coleman introduced his own definition of social capital by fusing the economic and the social streams together, embracing a more inclusive understanding of the term.[4]

Although the understandings behind social capital have diverged in several other ways, two components have remained a central focus of study in the wider body of social studies literature—namely, networks and social trust. Probably the most prominent scholar to emphasize the importance of capital exchange embedded in social networks is Ronald Burt, who defines social capital as both "the resources contacts hold and the structure of contacts in a network."[5] Burt argues that gains can be better appropriated in terms of access to "structural holes" in the competitive arena.[6] Because structural holes are points of disconnections between actors, they function as opportunities for information flow.

In the 1990s, political scientist Robert Putnam popularized the concept of social capital and gave it a wider sociological platform. In his seminal work *Bowling Alone*, Putnam affirmed that "social capital refers to connections among individuals—social networks and the norms of reciprocity and trustworthiness that arise from them."[7] By comparing social capital to "civic virtue," Putnam asserted that at the core of social capital is the idea that social

2. Granovetter, "Strength of Weak Ties," 205.

3. Bourdieu, "Forms of Capital," 241–58.

4. Coleman, "Social Capital," 95–120.

5. Burt, *Structural Holes*, 12.

6. Burt, *Structural Holes*, 1.

7. Putnam, *Bowling Alone*, 19.

networks matter for two reasons.[8] First, social networks provide internal returns, offering value to those who are a part of them. Second, such networks also produce external effects as a public good (e.g., lowering crime rates in a neighborhood). This understanding led to the distinction between *bonding* and *bridging* social capital. Bonding social capital brings people together who are like one another in various respects (ethnicity, gender, age, social class, etc.) and focuses on the networks *within* the community. Bridging social capital, on the other hand, refers to social networks that link people who are different from each other *across* communities.[9]

Quite provocatively, Putnam claimed that civic participation across the United States had been waning and that consequently, social capital had atrophied.[10] The idea that modernization and industrialization had undermined community bonds contributed to his drastic conclusions. Putnam attributed the apparent erosion of social capital to several social factors, such as urbanization and the emergence of two-career families. In addition, the culprit behind such decline had two immutable faces: technological innovation and generational replacement.[11]

Researchers in the mass communication field reacted negatively to Putnam's conclusions, arguing that it was not technology itself that was eroding social capital, but the time spent with it.[12] Further research found that the type of media use was an important variable in determining its relationship to social capital. As Littau observed, "The nature of the use and the type of content, then, are better predictors of social capital generation or erosion than the actual medium itself."[13] In a later work, *Better Together*, Putnam and Feldstein noted that a "new social capital" is "being created in interesting ways in many places and situations."[14] In

---

8. Putnam, *Bowling Alone*, 20.

9. Putnam, *Bowling Alone*, 22.

10. Putnam, *Bowling Alone*, 31–33.

11. Putnam, *Bowling Alone*, 275.

12. Littau, "Virtual Social Capital," 26.

13. Littau, "Virtual Social Capital," 26.

14. Putnam and Feldstein, *Better Together*, 4.

this work, Putnam and Feldstein provided "social capital success stories,"[15] hoping to signal the reemergence of social capital in new ways to rebuild social relationships. Putnam and Feldstein discussed many of the ways in which Americans were "making progress on the perennial challenge of re-creating new forms of community,"[16] which represents a more contemporary assessment of the current situation than the dreary portrait Putnam painted in *Bowling Alone.*

Concerned with the significant change in the American religious landscape, social conditions plaguing the country, and Putnam's remarks regarding the decline of social capital, Wuthnow contends that while certain kinds of civic engagement may be in decline, innovative forms are actually emerging and replacing traditional activities. Wuthnow argues that Americans are "experimenting with looser, more sporadic, ad hoc connections in place of the long-term memberships in hierarchical organizations of the past."[17] Because social institutions, such as the church, have become more porous and fragmented, "instead of cultivating lifelong ties with their neighbors, or joining organizations that reward faithful long-term service, people come together around specific needs."[18] These needs can be met in a multiplicity of ways, such as partnering with community agencies focused on serving and providing individuals with information and resources who may not have access to capital.

Social Capital and the Church

Social researchers have long recognized that congregations are among the producers of social capital.[19] For instance, Nancy Ammerman observes that what "congregations contribute to the social

15. Putnam and Feldstein, *Better Together,* 5.

16. Putnam and Feldstein, *Better Together,* 6.

17. Wuthnow, *Loose Connections,* 5.

18. Wuthnow, *Loose Connections,* 9.

19. See Ammerman, *Congregation and Community*; Wuthnow, *Boundless Faith.*

order is not unique."[20] That is, congregations, like any other civic organization, provide spaces for belonging and a venue for the formation of relational ties. Wuthnow also shows that congregations not only serve as formal service providers, but as spaces where social ties can help meet needs informally.[21] In other words, the kind of social capital that a congregation is more likely to generate is the bonding type, by strengthening social ties among the members.

Although most of the discussion on religious social capital has focused on the congregation as its source *par excellence*, a few more recent studies have acknowledged the role that transnational religious connections play in the creation of social capital.[22] As new patterns of global connectedness in the church begin to emerge, a fresh trend has slowly settled—mutually beneficial partner relationships. In fact, American congregations seeking to enter into partnerships with congregations from other parts of the world, create channels through which resources, ideas, personnel, and information can flow.[23] Because partnerships are built upon trustworthy relationships, entail mutuality, and operate on the bedrock of exchange, their structure lends itself to be a natural reservoir of social capital.

In recent decades, as a result of globalization and relatively inexpensive travel, American churches have proactively participated in transcultural activities with more affordability and accessibility. Among the far-reaching implications for contemporary missions is the idea that healthy congregational partnerships offer an opportunity to display unity and engage in collaborative efforts amongst Christians of differing social class, economic status, or denominational affiliations. In fact, Wuthnow asserts that "the situation in which American church members now find themselves is one of unprecedented opportunities for engagement in

---

20. Ammerman, *Congregation and Community*, 362.

21. Wuthnow, "Saving America?" 83.

22. See Brown, "Friendship Is Forever;" Priest, "Peruvian Churches;" Wesley, *A Common Mission*.

23. Wuthnow, *Boundless Faith*, 139.

the experiences of people whose lives are quite different from their own."[24] Partnering with other organizations or churches will create more social capital, and therefore a richer possibility for the realization of the Kingdom.

As already discussed, social capital works under the assumption that reciprocal ties of trust bring about mutual benefit. For that reason, partnerships offer a promising framework by which different resources may be shared and channeled to fulfill the various needs existing in the specific contexts of the partners. Because partners bring different types of resources, experiences, and information with them, these should flow both ways. Whereas partners with financial resources might be able to aid those with less, partners with more intangible goods, such as vision and fervor, might be able to share some of their ideas with the other. Missional partnerships and intentional relationships with others along different social strata may uncover the richest well of social capital available, dug by the inspiring vision of ecclesial institutions coming together for a common good.

Social Life in the Virtual World

With the advent of the online community, social media, and technological communication, an increasing number of research studies have discussed the many ways in which social capital can be generated and availed through these venues. In an early study, Wellman et al. found that individuals tend to engage with online sites as a way to replace absent interactions in their daily lives, seeking a suitable environment for connections that seem to be lacking in the real world.[25]

Technology has powerfully changed how society operates. Technology can be used to interact with individuals from all over the world, which in turn can influence and shape perspectives, culture, and society in general. Entire virtual communities have

24. Wuthnow, *Boundless Faith*, 20.

25. Wellman et al., "Computer Networks," 213–38.

been formed around open-access blogging, topics of interests, private groups, and social networking sites.[26] The Internet creates bonding social capital, connecting people with similar interests, beliefs, and life experiences. It also creates bridging social capital, bringing people from different socio-economic groups together virtually through online forum chats, social media groups, or blogs.[27] The Internet will continue to provide great options for social connection and interaction as well as for information flow and exchange of goods, such as the ones provided through Facebook's marketplace.

Research studies assessing the influence, impact, and role of social media in the church have been surfacing in recent years. A few articles have reflected on the opportunities that social media can offer the church to advance its mission. For instance, Singarayar recognized the great possibilities that forms of social media offer to the church, stating that they have "emerged as powerful and efficient tools for sharing information, shaping opinions, connecting people across geographical domains and cultures."[28] Moreover, research was conducted among Ghanaian pastors to assess the potential that virtual platforms such as Facebook could present for advancing their mission. The study revealed that the pastors were followed by individuals of diverse religious backgrounds, presenting more opportunities for dialogue, connection, and outreach beyond their geographical location.[29] More research is necessary to understand the conditions and effects inherent in virtual communities, online congregations, and social media to provide individuals who might be unable to physically attend church services with a sense of belonging that is often sought through in-person attendance.

26. See Gillmor, *We the Media.*

27. Lin, *Social Capital,* 210.

28. Singarayar, "Social Media," 791–95.

29. White et al., "Missional Study," 1–8.

Online Networking Sites

For the church to generate, mobilize and utilize social capital through the virtual world, it must not only consider the unique opportunities that these platforms present but must also learn how to better utilize them. Online platforms and virtual villages can provide a venue for bonding and bridging social capital, as well as meeting cognitive needs (information and interests), emotional needs (interaction and connection), social needs (entertainment and escape), and even financial needs (through fundraisers such as GoFundMe). The church should explore new ways in which these needs can be met. Social networks possess an incredible amount of resources and access to individuals and their connections that would not be available anywhere else, or with the incredible reach that virtual groups and communities possess.

As an example, let us consider "OptionB" (an entity that provides resources for navigating grief) founded by Sheryl Sandberg. To help people build resilience in the midst of difficulty and adversity, this organization has created a space where individuals can share their stories with others facing a similar situation (whether it be grief and loss, illness, abuse, divorce, or family challenges) through their website (OptionB.org) and via Facebook. The private groups, open to subscribers on Facebook, claim over 850,000 followers, with 42,000 active members in the "coping with grief" group as of 2023. The church too can invest strategically in these types of endeavors as individuals around the world experience the effects of change, crisis, and chaos in order to minister to individuals facing life-altering challenges.

The Internet is a culture in and of itself. Understanding the Internet as a virtual platform for social engagement and a hyper-medium that heightens the speed by which communication takes place, the church must learn to utilize it wisely. Acquiring competence in this area will provide a way for the church to maximize its opportunities, be a peaceful presence, reach out to others with kindness, and use its voice to placate the volatility of inflammatory conversations. By applying cross-cultural principles as if the

Internet is the equivalent of a culture that needs contextualization, the church might find a way to better utilize this platform as a means to influence others. On one hand, witnessing through social media may become a way to serve as a mediating presence amidst the cacophony of voices that seem to compete for people's attention. On the other hand, the overuse of social media, increased dependence on technologies, and the digital revolution have brought about negative consequences that must be addressed with equal weight.

Cultural trends such as the rise of electronic communication and digital media have long-lasting consequences. Research shows that the rise of digital media has had a huge impact on mental health. According to a recent study conducted by a San Diego team of psychology researchers, rates of major depressive disorder and mood disorders have been increasing at a steady rate since 2017, all related to the use of social media.[30] Other studies have found a positive correlation between the use of social media and sleep disturbance among youth, while yet another set of studies revealed that people spending more time on social media and less time with others face-to-face reported lower well-being and higher rates of suicide.[31] To avoid these serious threats, we must not permit the use of digital media to replace face-to-face interaction and relationships.

Addressing this situation must be at the forefront of missionary training. Adequate access to mental health care should be encouraged to combat the unintended effects of the cyber world. Equipping the church with tools and skills will make Christians more fully aware of the opportunities the virtual world offers while also preparing them to minimize its ills. Certainly, technology developments can aid the church in advancing the Kingdom, but they can also lead to poor stewardship through excessive use and cause emotional and psychological distress. While the development of online communities and virtual platforms has presented new opportunities to reach the world with the gospel, its overuse

30. Twenge, "Age, Period, and Cohort," 185.

31. Twenge, "Age, Period, and Cohort," 185.

may take a toll. There is no better way to maximize the benefits of the virtual world and minimize its unintended consequences than by being embedded in a community of faith where interactions happen face-to-face and social media platforms can be duly utilized to make connections and reach out to others.

4

Making Room for the Nones

THIS CHAPTER EXAMINES THE current trend of the religious unaffiliated, along with the cultural shifts taking place among younger generations that lie behind their reluctance to affiliate with a particular Christian tradition. Because most religiously unaffiliated people come from the younger generational cohorts, it is natural to conclude that the digital revolution might be contributing to this decline. As this chapter will show, several factors are contributing to the decline in religious affiliation in the United States. One of them is the church's seeming irrelevance to daily life and its reluctance to address pertinent social issues. As a result, some have lost interest in organized religion, even if they grew up in church, and are now "prodigals." Others might identify as Christians but do not profess to belong to any specific religious group and prefer to be "nomads."

The wave of religious disaffiliation that began in the 1990s in the United States has gone from *a* concern to perhaps *the* concern of church leaders. In the last decade, disaffiliation has become so widespread that it is now recognized as a perceived threat to the existence and longevity of the church. As younger generations continue to lose interest in the church and religious affiliation continues its steady decline, the church must turn to a relational approach to bear faithful witness to the gospel among these populations.

Examining the Trend

Religion in the West and Christianity in particular have been on a steady decline for the last few decades. In the latter half of the nineteenth century, secularization theory was born—namely, the belief that with the onset of modernization and urbanization, religion would cease to shape values and influence societal norms, becoming confined to the private sphere of life. This theory was built on the premises of the Enlightenment period, during which it was assumed that human reason could establish a perfect society. During this age, advances in science, technology, and education seemed to offer a way to replace the perceived "unverifiable" beliefs associated with religion. A century after the promulgation of the secularization theory, sociologists realized that religion had not vanished from the global spectrum. In fact, the creation of new religious movements in the West, the proliferation of Pentecostalism that drew the masses into its churches in the Global South, and a growing interest in mystical and spiritual experiences have continued to draw people back to the religious world.

Despite this growing trend and renewed interest in the spiritual dimension, religious affiliation has not followed the same trajectory. Many studies have examined this trend, calling the unaffiliated "the nones" due to their status of having no religious preference. According to a Pew Research Center study, the percentage of Americans who claim no particular religious affiliation has increased from 22.8% in 2014 to 29% in 2021, and the majority of these belong to young generations.[1] A quick glimpse at the statistics by generational cohort reveals that Generation Z is considered the least religious generation in American history, with 34% claiming no affiliation to religious traditions, compared to 29% of Millennials, who rank second.[2]

Several studies have illumined the social identity of the nones and why they insist on staying away from organized religion. One

---

1. Smith, "About Three-in-Ten."
2. Cox, "Generation Z."

such study utilizes the concept of *liminality*[3] to describe the state of the nones as those standing halfway in and halfway out of religious identity, perhaps likely to change their position.[4] The study argues that many nones still hold a weak tie to some particular religious tradition and may occasionally identify with that tradition, but they prefer to steer away from becoming members of any particular religious group. This position holds that the majority of nones, rather than being secular, are actually liminal and thus their position may change with the passing of time. This liminality creates significant difficulty in adequately assessing the participants' degree of affiliation.[5] Research conducted by the Pew Center corroborates this assumption, indicating that 74% of unaffiliated adults were raised with religious affiliation and that their disaffiliation happened later in life.[6] If secularization were the culprit behind this dramatic shift, other indicators would be present as well, such as a significant decrease in influence that religion has held in the social arena or the important role that religion has played in people's lives. But by and large, this has not been the case. Religious beliefs have not ceased to impact how people perceive reality, and their lack of support for religious institutions seems to be for reasons other than loss of belief in God.

James White, in his seminal work *The Rise of the Nones*, affirms this idea. White asserts that though the nones do not claim to be religious, they still believe in God and consider themselves spiritual.[7] In fact, about a quarter of American adults (27%) view themselves as "spiritual but not religious."[8] Their lack of affiliation does not reflect disinterest in spiritual matters, but reveals deeper

---

3. The term "liminality" has been borrowed from cultural anthropologist Victor Turner, who uses it to refer to the middle stage of a ritual process in which the person redefines his identity in terms of ambiguity while passing through a realm that has few or none of the attributes of the past or future stages.

4. Lim et al., "Secular and Liminal," 597.

5. Lim et al., "Secular and Liminal," 599.

6. Pew, "Nones on the Rise," 16.

7. White, *The Rise*, 21.

8. Lipka and Gecewicz, "More Americans."

concerns with religion itself. Another Pew Research Center report found that one-third of the unaffiliated say religion is somewhat important and two-thirds claim strong beliefs in God.[9] Young adults are likely to share beliefs about life after death and the existence of heaven, hell, and miracles, with an increased emphasis on the supernatural, the mystical, and the magical.

Factors Affecting Religious Affiliation

Given the trajectory that religious affiliation has taken, several questions arise. What lies behind the nones' lack of desire to formally affiliate with a religious organization? What are the reasons for such a drastic shift? One factor contributing to the shift seems to be the perception that religion is often aligned with conservative politics and that religious people tend to cast judgment on sexual minorities. Two sociologists concluded from an analytical study of survey data that there is a link between conservative political views among the religious and the decrease of religious affiliation among youth.[10] Their research suggests that the association between conservative politics and religion has pushed some moderates and most liberals with weak religious ties away from Christianity altogether.[11] Therefore, it is likely that many young adults may choose to not affiliate with a religious organization because of that organization's traditional and conservative views. Putnam and Campbell note that young Americans have come to view religion as "judgmental, homophobic, hypocritical, and too political."[12] Furthermore, they assert that young people's views on homosexuality and gay marriage are in conflict with religious ideals that advocate more conservative positions, leading to their disaffiliation with conservative traditions.[13] In her research, missiologist

9. Pew, "Nones on the Rise," 12.

10. Hout and Fischer, "Why More Americans," 3–4.

11. Hout and Fischer, "Why More Americans," 14.

12. Putnam and Campbell, *American Grace*, 121.

13. Putnam and Campbell, *American Grace*, 120–30.

Beth Seversen found that when churches are silent on significant social issues young adults unconsciously absorb the message that the church is not fully interested in addressing current contextual realities. She writes, "When it comes to socio-political topics such as race, ethnicity, gender, and political struggles—including significant social issues involving economic and educational disparity, white supremacy, mass incarceration, mistreatment of immigrants, police shootings, violence against black youth, and human trafficking—silence is understood to mean "We don't care."[14] Ryan Burge, a political scientist, also affirms that "disaffiliation is directly related to political ideology," although he believes that determining the direction of the cause-effect relationship is difficult.[15]

Notwithstanding, political views cannot account for the loss of religious affiliation alone. Other possible reasons have been identified as root causes of this decline. A study conducted by the Psychology Department of San Diego State University describes the impact of social influences, such as individualism, religious pluralism, and the clash between verifiable facts (science) and ungrounded ideologies (faith), as additional reasons behind this drastic shift.[16] The level of individualism in a society affects the conceptions of values in such society. And individualism seems to play a role in processing personal decisions apart from considering how it affects communal values embedded in religious systems or family traditions. Furthermore, people have lost trust in many religious institutions due to sexual scandals and have been repulsed by the manner in which some ecclesial communities have handled them.[17]

Apart from political differences and the decline of social trust, the growing tendency of younger populations toward technology, seen more clearly through the use of social media platforms, smartphones, and online activities, has led them to a lack of

---

14. Seversen, *Not Done Yet*, 107.

15. Burge, *The Nones*, 52–53.

16. Twenge, "Generational," 14.

17. Burge, *The Nones*, 58–61.

inability to focus on other matters. These "digital natives," mostly represented by Gen Z, the youngest generation in America, were born and raised in a technological world with digital fingers, where TikTok, YouTube and Facebook have always been a part of their lives. These platforms offer venues for socialization and exchange of information that can naturally contribute to disengagement with religion, as they prefer to find connections at their fingertips.

Generational Influences

Every generation displays general and unique traits. The political, economic, social, and technological influences of the culture in which people are raised exert a lasting impact on their identity formation and collective values. Different effects associated with how a generation processes life experiences and determine cultural values should be taken into account. Although these are not exclusive, they are significant to understand how a generation shapes and regulates its value system. First is the "age effect," which encompass all the events associated with changes typical of age and plays a determining role in how people deal with social change. Second is the "period effect," which comprises all global events that affect all generations simultaneously, influencing the attitudes and behaviors of individuals differently based on their experiences, attitudes, and understandings of these events (such as the technology revolution). Finally is the "cohort effect," which includes all historical events experienced and remembered by a single generation more than others (such as a world war or economic recession), impacting the level of personal and social consciousness.[18] All these effects shape the value system of generational cohorts and impact the manner in which life is lived and experiences are processed.

An important distinction must be noted with regard to particular behaviors, where certain values might be interpreted as indicators of age rather than being generational in nature, leading us

18. Ruspini, in *An Introduction to Longitudinal Research*, describes these effects as actions involved in processing social change.

to conclude that young people could subscribe to more traditional practices once they age. But when it comes to religion, research suggests that religious affiliation seems to be a generational trend. A study compared data from 11 million adolescents between 13 and 18 years of age from 1966 and 2014, showing that younger generations tend to be less religious. The study concluded that the "lesser religious orientation is not due to their youth, but instead to their generation and the particular time period" in which they live.[19] In other words, attitudes toward organized religion cannot be attributed to being young necessarily, but to shifts in cultural values shared collectively by a generational cohort.

Shifts in Social Values

Examining America's youngest generations will provide a glimpse as to how current events shape their collective identity. A recent research study characterizes Gen Zs as the most diverse generation yet and as a "highly collaborative cohort that cares deeply about others and has a pragmatic attitude about how to address a set of inherited issues like climate change."[20] Furthermore, the authors of *Gen Z, Explained* describe this generation as extraordinarily thoughtful, promising, and perceptive, while not ignoring the larger issues that have led them to be "deeply pessimistic about the problems they have inherited: climate change, violence, racial and gender injustice, failures of the political system, and little chance of owning a home or improving on their parents' level of affluence."[21] It is evident that the diversity so prevalent in younger generations may make them more naturally aware of and inclined to fight for marginalized groups of people, concerns that have been often dismissed by older generations who have not been exposed to such diversity and/or by traditional religious groups that have failed to adequately address them. Both Millennials and Gen Zs are diverse,

19. Twenge, "Generational," 15.

20. De Witte, "Gen Z are not 'Coddled.'"

21. Katz et al., "Gen Z, Explained," 4.

and as a result, their views on racial issues have also become less partisan. These generations have less interest in maintaining the status quo, and they are less reluctant to make social connections that go beyond their social groups.

With the speed of high-tech advancements and the plethora of networking sites, Millennials and Gen Zs have a tremendous advantage over previous generations who were confined to smaller social circles and a more traditional socialization process. For younger generations, fulfillment is still found in connecting with others face-to-face, but perhaps of even greater importance is the possibility of virtual interconnectedness with people from all over the world and from various backgrounds. As a result, the young are more likely to hold a less biased view toward other ethnicities or races as they become exposed to a wide range of cultures throughout the virtual world. The fact that 39% of Millennials are represented by minorities while 89% of white Americans age 18 to 25 support interracial relationships may confirm this idea.[22]

Another peculiar and prevalent shift among younger generations is their ability to express themselves in unique ways. Posting videos online, engaging in TikTok, and having body tattoos are ways in which younger generations highlight their uniqueness. Their self-expression, however, is not limited to the physical dimension. In recent years, a surge of secular movements has drawn the attention of thousands of Millennials and Gen Zs with the intention of providing a space to share life with others in nontraditional ways.

One such movement is "Burning Man," an annual event in northern Nevada dedicated to community, art, self-reliance, and self-expression. Launched in 1986 with a gathering of only twenty individuals, this event boasted nearly 70,000 in attendance in 2021. Among the ten guiding principles, created to serve as a reflection of the community's ethos, are the following: radical inclusion, gifting, radical self-reliance, radical self-expression, communal effort, and participation.[23] A quick look at the Burning Man website shows

22. Pew, "Changing Religious Landscape," 16.

23. Burning Man, "What Is Burning Man?"

that over the last few years, about 62% of the participants were Millennials and Gen Zs while 73% of all participants reported no religious affiliation, which seems pretty standard when compared to theattendance over the last ten years.[24] This event provides an outlet for younger generations to share their innovative skills, make social connections with like-minded individuals, and express themselves in contemporary ways. Burning Man exemplifies the prototype of an ideal religion, offering much while demanding little.

Younger generations are also highly educated. Younger Millennials and most Gen Zs seem more open to nontraditional delivery systems of education and other alternatives, such as professional trades or YouTube tutorials to gain free expertise in a particular area. Despite the fact that younger Millennials have not yet finished their formal education, they may be on track to become the most educated generation in the history of the United States.[25] Because Millennials grew up in times of greater stability than Gen Zs, they were able to carry out their educational pursuits with less anxiety. On the other hand, because external crises and virtual explorations have greatly affected the mental health of younger generations, members of Gen Z have been more reluctant to embrace long-term commitments.

Although the church's prospects for the future may look dim in light of these growing trends, these developments have also awakened the church to be more proactive in their engagement with younger generations and its outreach efforts. It has often fallen to the fields of science and religion to provide mechanisms by which individuals may be aided in the process of finding solutions or answers to their needs. But in the age of rapid technological advancement, the key question is this: What will religion offer that technology is incapable of providing? Answering this question by taking into consideration the value systems of young generations

24. See https://burningman.org/about/history/brc-history/census-data/ for a complete history, timeline, and census that tracks changes in population and attitudes of event participants.

25. Pew, "Changing Religious Landscape," 49.

is the task facing any religious organization, system or group that wishes to bring disconnected, unengaged, and disinterested Millennials and Gen Zs back to church. It may well be that, in the midst of its current apparent weakness and decline in the West, religion could soon rediscover a stronger pulse in the days ahead.

Friendship as Witness

One of the most significant and indispensable ways in which Christians can be effective in their witness to younger generations who are losing interest in organized religion is by intentionally building relationships with them. As Jeff Stark clearly states, this can only happen when "we go out, making our life's calling our proximity to and presence with those searching for a hope they can't seem to articulate."[26] When we are in close proximity with those who profess no religion or claim no religious affiliation, we become aware of their deepest needs and the roots of their disappointments. Those who have walked away from religion or might not be interested in religious teachings at all might change their posture if, rather than seeking to invite them into a way of life, they are invited into our lives first. Beth Seversen's research agrees. She says, "for relationships to be transformative and for invitations to be sincere, friendships need to be genuine."[27] There is no better way to break down the walls of indifference than by opening doors that welcome difference.

The Christian community cannot be committed just to itself; it must be committed to *people*, to their growth and inner freedom, to their interests and dilemmas, and to the totality of their being. These features can be nurtured only in an environment of friendship. In a true community of people committed to people rather than to ideologies, love transcends the boundaries of the community to effect change outside of it. People who have walked away from religion, as research has shown, have done so because

26. Stark, *The News Is Good*, 18.

27. Seversen, *Not Done Yet*, 33.

religious teachings do not seem applicable or relevant to their daily lives. In other cases, people cannot rationally make sense of religious beliefs or ideas as they often seem to be at odds with a scientific world. Dialogue about the gospel message can bear fruit only in fertile ground that has been cultivated in the context of friendship. After all, the essence of Christianity does not rely primarily on the capacity to *persuade* someone, but on the ability to *relate* to someone. Our love for people can be complete only when the views and perceptions we have held about people are dismantled by the very encounters we have with them. A true *community* of faith becomes a community of *faith* when the community remains open to the outsider and grows in love toward them. And it is there, in the tension of differing perspectives, that the good news of Jesus might find a way to remind us all that he is the true light of life illumining the way (John 8:12).

True friendship learns the secret of listening. Many people are looking for an ear that will simply listen. Sadly, these individuals do not often find it among Christians, because Christians are more interested in talking rather than in choosing to sit with people who need a listening ear. Dietrich Bonhoeffer affirms, "We should listen with the ears of God that we may speak the Word of God."[28] Christine Pohl supports this same idea—"Often, the best gift we can give another person is our time and attention."[29] The nonreligious and unaffiliated might not be prepared to hear what the Scriptures have to say, but they might entertain the possibility of hearing it one day if they see it lived out in front of them first.

In the hostile world in which we live, we need a new kind of apologetics. This type of apologetics can no longer be based on a rationalistic explanation of religious concepts nor on a simplistic presentation of theological principles. While one should always be ready to give answers to those who ask us to provide reasons for our belief, the truth of the matter is that most people are no longer asking for reasons. They are wondering if they will ever see the evidence. Thus, apologetics in today's world should include a keen

28. Bonhoeffer, *Life Together*, 99.

29. Pohl, *Living into Community*, 170.

ability to engage with the unengaged and a genuine move to step into the lives of people who are waiting to meet the real Jesus in the faces of his followers.

But apologetics for Gen Zs runs deeper than answering new questions. One of the most pressing need of young nones is that they are spiritually illiterate and, consequently, lack a metanarrative that can provide stability and purpose. To fill this unfortunate gap in a post-Christian world, many are turning to the occult or to science for transcendent meaning.[30] Sociologist Pitrim Sorokin argued that civilizations tend to fluctuate between two directions: the ideational (more spiritual) and the sensate (more rational). In its struggle with the search for transcendental realities, much of the modern world is leaning toward the ideational side, where the search for an experience outweighs the need to find rational explanations for reality.[31] This vacuum provides an opportunity for presenting a gospel that is authentic and sensitive to the power of the Spirit.

The need to create experiences goes beyond the spiritual realm, however. The arts and popular culture are another place where younger generations are finding meaning and connection. Ted Turnau, in *Popologetics*, argues that "Christians who want to reach out to their non-Christian friends and neighbors need a worldview-oriented approach, an approach that deals with the popular culture in all its complicated, messed-up glory."[32] Turnau believes that engaging the other where they are and learning about their interests will open doors for dialogue so that Christians can speak into their lives with credibility. Popular culture can fill one's need for social connections only at the surface level, however. Everyone seeks relational connections, but mature believers are needed to engage with non-Christians at deeper levels without falling into waves of moral relativism and worldly influence.

Dana Roberts recognizes that "modern society is experiencing a friendship crisis of epic proportions" where an estimated

30. White, *Meet Generation Z*, 132.

31. White, *Meet Generation Z*, 132.

32. Turnau, *Popologetics*, 11.

twenty percent of Americans confess that they are lonely.[33] I am reminded of the words of English poet William Blake: "The bird: a nest, the spider: a web, man: friendship." These simple words may be interpreted in many different ways, but one way is to see them as describing how the bird, the spider, and humans find comfort and meaning and feel at home in what they build. Just as the bird builds a nest, the spider builds a web, and man builds a friendship, so will their existence be sustained by virtue of the care they devote to that which they have built.

But there is indeed a crisis of friendship, primarily driven by human division, busyness in life, and fragmentation in relationships. Many studies have indicated that "friendship is the most important single force" behind people choosing to become Christians.[34] But friendship can only be a form of witness if it is built on a strong friendship with Jesus first. "Being friends with Jesus within the worldwide community of faith," Roberts notes, "is a missional practice that witnesses to the reign of God."[35] The Great Commandment in the Synoptic Gospels describes what our response should be to the grace of God as it operates in our lives: to love God and love others as ourselves (Matt 22:37–39, Mark 12:29–31, Luke 10:25–28). But in the Gospel of John, we find Jesus giving us a "new commandment." He encourages his disciples to love one another just as he loved them (John 13:34). The love of friendship that we have for each other, enabled by our friendship with Jesus, should also propel us to befriend the nones and seek to connect with them in their field of interest and where they are in life with the hope that they may see Jesus through us.

33. Roberts, *Faithful Friendships,* 1.

34. Kreider and Kreider, *Worship and Mission,* 223.

35. Roberts, *Faithful Friendships,* 15.

5

Breaking Religious Barriers

THE CHURCH'S MINISTRY INVOLVES not only engaging with those who claim no religious affiliation, but also dialoguing with those who adhere to a different set of religious beliefs. Missiologists have long considered the implications of crossing religious barriers and entering into dialogue as an opportunity to engage the religious other in amicable ways. In recent years, scholars have begun to rethink what it means to engage in mission in light of the rapidly changing movement of peoples around the globe. Rather than conceiving the primary task of the church in terms of mission *to* the nations, some missiologists are now framing it as mission *among* the nations.[1]

Despite these signs of hopeful discourse, interreligious interaction has often provoked controversy, led to disputes, and become one of the most inflammatory issues within Christian circles. While evangelicals have remained steady in their position that conversion should be the goal of mission, some mainline Protestants have advocated for a more inclusive spirituality that embraces non-Christian religions on equal ground. Despite differences within the Christian community, learning to approach and engage the religious other may be one of the most important frontiers that Christians must learn to bridge. It would be easier

1. Bevans, "Prophetic," 7.

to remain isolated from other religious traditions, but Christ has given us the higher calling of loving our neighbor, which includes those who profess a different set of beliefs.

Christian Views Toward Other Religions

When we consider approaches to individuals who claim to belong to a different religious group, it becomes important to understand the motives behind our evangelistic efforts (or the lack thereof). Traditionally, three general categories have been used to describe Christian perspectives toward other religions: exclusivism, inclusivism and pluralism.[2] These categories represent only three major points along a broad spectrum of Christian approaches, which I have described more fully elsewhere.[3] In theological considerations of world religions, evangelicals have generally focused on questions of truth and salvation rather than on matters of revelation.[4] The issue of ultimate truth and salvation has become a point of contention between evangelicals and those holding to more liberal Christian views. Does God save everyone regardless of their religious beliefs? Does God save those who have had the full revelation of his being through the person of Christ Jesus as well as those who have never heard of him? Or will only those who have repented and made a profession of faith enter into paradise?

These questions cannot be answered hastily, and it is far beyond the scope of this chapter to answer them comprehensively. Here, the intent is to survey the positions and views within Christianity that have resulted from different soteriological understandings. To begin, most evangelicals have taken the exclusivist position, affirming three "nonnegotiables."[5] First, the authority and final supremacy of Jesus Christ represent the normative standard by which other claims to revelation must be assessed. Second,

---

2. McDermott and Netland, *A Trinitarian Theology*, 12.

3. See Twibell, "Interreligious Dialogue."

4. Clarke, "Dialogue or Diatribe," 25.

5. Tennent, *Christianity at the Religious Roundtable*, 16–17.

the Christian faith must be centered on the proclamation of the Christ event. Third, salvation comes through repentance and faith in the redemptive work of Christ, and no one can be saved apart from him. Among proponents of this view are Hendrick Kraemer[6] and Ronald Nash.[7] While advocating these three nonnegotiables, exclusivists also hold that God provides truths about himself and humanity through general revelation that may be present in other world religions. Such general revelation may thus provide points of continuity as long as it is consistent with biblical revelation, a view advocated by Gerald McDermott and Harold Netland.[8]

Inclusivists, while affirming the first two aforementioned nonnegotiables held by exclusivists, differ slightly in their understanding of the final point. For inclusivists, the redeeming work of Christ on the cross is *ontologically* necessary but not *epistemologically* necessary. In other words, one need not know about Christ to receive the grace offered through his work on the cross. Inclusivism articulates a soteriology based on universal access, claiming that people who are not cognizant of the gospel of Christ can be saved if they are aware of God and move toward him through general revelation.[9] Among the proponents of this position are Catholic theologian Karl Rahner[10] and Protestant theologian Clark Pinnock.[11]

Pluralists, on the other hand, reject all three nonnegotiables. While affirming that every world religion provides a path toward salvation, pluralists also maintain that conflicting truth claims can be reconciled by taking an experiential rather than a normative vantage point. For example, John Hick, a prominent proponent of religious pluralism, believes that religions "embody different perceptions and conceptions of, and correspondingly different

---

6. See Pitman, *Twentieth Century* where he describes in length Kraemer's hard exclusivism.

7. See Nash, *Is Jesus the Only Savior?*

8. See McDermott and Netland, *A Trinitarian Theology.*

9. Ott et al., *Encountering Theology of Missions,* 298.

10. See Rahner, *Spirit in the World.*

11. See Pinnock, *A Wideness in God's Mercy.*

responses to, the Real from within the major variant ways of being human."[12] By "Real," Hick means the ineffable transcendental category that religions use to describe the ultimate reality, which might be personal (Holy Trinity, Allah, or Yahweh) or impersonal (Brahman, Tao, or Dhamarkaya). According to most pluralists, Christianity is just one of many religions that provide access to salvation and therefore should not be perceived as holding any final authority over other belief systems.

For the committed Christian who believes that God has made provision for salvation through Jesus Christ, Hick's stance presents some difficulties. First, contrary to his understanding, the Real can be known through the particularity of the Christ event, as the Real is uniquely knowable through the concrete expression of Jesus who is the exact representation of God. Second, although Hick is right that religions embody different perceptions and conceptions of the Real, these religions do not express partial revelation that is complementary to each other. In fact, in some cases, they contradict each other. Finally, although Hick claims that the ineffable reality of the transcendental realm is the focal point which all religious people are trying to reach, Christianity is about the story of God, and his story is about salvation history. In this story, Christ becomes the point of climax and the pinnacle of God's salvific purposes where God comes down from his throne to be with us, unlike in any other religious story.

Moving the Discussion Forward

What, then, should be the way forward? One recent approach has been proposed by Amos Yong, a Malaysian-American theologian, whose "pneumatological approach"[13] goes beyond a Christocentric paradigm to locate the Holy Spirit as a cosmic divine presence that extends beyond ecclesiastical boundaries. Yong maintains that rather than framing the discussion around Christology, a

12. Hick, *An Interpretation*, 240.

13. Clarke, "Dialogue or Diatribe," 30.

"foundational pneumatology" should be the basis by which to interpret the role of the Spirit as he moves beyond the ecclesial body. That is, one must see God, self, and the world in a way that is inspired by the movement of the Spirit.[14] In short, Yong argues that the particularities of the Christ event must be heightened by the universality of the Spirit. This approach is helpful as it emphasizes the power of God to draw people to himself through the Spirit in ways we may not be fully aware of, leaving such outcomes ultimately in his hands. Dismissing this possibility could lead to a fundamentalist perspective in which we claim the right to be the final arbiters. Nevertheless, Yong's approach has also received a fair share of criticism, particularly due to his inherent lack of Christocentric focus.

Timothy Tennent remains convinced that Christology must be at the center of the discussion. He proposes that "the way forward is to embrace our convictions regarding the truthfulness and uniqueness of the Christian gospel while fully engaging in honest, open interactions with members of other religious traditions."[15] Tennent suggests the term "engaged exclusivist"[16] as an alternative approach for the evangelical encountering the religious other. That is, while affirming the three nonnegotiables that most evangelicals hold, Christians should also emphasize an open stance regarding general revelation and seek to become missiologically prepared to engage others where they are. Tennent believes that despite the complexities at play, Christians can maintain and express their faith without having to suspend their own convictions in the process.

Salvation can be found only in and through Jesus Christ, and salvation is a matter of God's infinite grace. With that in mind, another approach, known as "non-restrictivist exclusivism," has emerged.[17] This label suggests that it is not possible to determine the destiny of people who have not been evangelized. Therefore, we should leave their destiny "in the hands of the all-just and

14. Clarke, "Dialogue or Diatribe," 30.

15. Tennent, *Christianity*, 26.

16. Tennent, *Christianity*, 26.

17. Stott and Wright, *Christian Mission*, 178.

all-merciful God" while affirming that the path to God is through Jesus Christ.[18] Christopher Wright is a proponent of this view, who more specifically argues that God's salvation is *exclusively* accomplished by the atoning death and victorious resurrection of Jesus Christ, and, therefore, there is no other basis on which any human being can be saved. However, God's saving grace is not *restricted* to the limits of our evangelistic success or failure. Wright affirms that there is no salvation in other religions because religion does not have an inherent power to save anybody. Salvation belongs to God.[19]

General Revelation

With regard to the revelation of God, God has not left himself without witness in places and religious systems where Christ's presence has not yet been made known. Surely, God provides the means by which the cosmic renewal of creation may be restored through Christ and the Spirit, but even those outside the realm of the knowledge of his salvation are given a type of *logos spermatikos* (a seed of reason) so that they are not left without excuse (Rom 1:20). That is, individuals who have not encountered the saving grace of God experientially can utilize reason to recognize the sovereignty of God through his created order. Does that mean that everyone will be ultimately saved? Surely, God wills that everyone come to repentance and that no one would perish (2 Pet 3:9). God is rich in mercy and desires that all people be saved and come to a knowledge of the truth (1 Tim 2:4). Yet God's grace and invitation require a response.

If the Spirit gives life and offers grace to every creature, it would seem reasonable to expect him to be present in the religious dimension of humanity as a whole, but there is no salvation in religion because only God saves. If God intends to reach the nations, it makes sense to think that he is already at work preveniently in

18. Stott and Wright, *Christian Mission*, 178.

19. See Wright, *Salvation Belongs to our God* for a fuller description of this view.

other faiths, to some extent. It seemed to be so for Cornelius, a non-Christian whose moral life was highly praised before he became a Christian (Acts 10:2). Similarly, Melchizedek, a king and priest outside of the Jewish faith, was greatly respected by Abraham and somehow already knew the "true God" (Gen 14:18–20). Certainly, it is one thing to recognize the work of God who moves outside of his people in ways to draw them to himself and quite another thing to see other faiths as means or vehicles of salvation. As Clark Pinnock says, "One can be sensitive to the Spirit among people of other faiths without minimizing real and crucial differences between them."[20] Even when Jesus is the ultimate revelation of God, the Spirit is at work everywhere preparing the way for Jesus to be made fully known. God counts on his people to partner with him in revealing Christ among the nations.

Dialogue as Mission

The emergence of a multi-cultural, multi-ethnic and multi-religious world makes dialogue fundamental to dismantle patterns of misunderstanding. Constructing bridges of careful discourse and making it a priority to engage the religious other with deep respect must be at the forefront of our agenda. John Stott has been a leading voice in framing interreligious dialogue as conversations "marked by authenticity, humility, integrity, and sensitivity."[21]

Although practices of interreligious dialogue are both ancient and modern, the last few decades have seen a plethora of new developments in this field, calling for the formation of authentic encounters between various religious traditions. One of the most recent efforts is R20, an inter-religious forum created in 2022 as part of the annual G20 international convocation. The Indonesian organization Nahdlatul Ulama (the largest Muslim civil society movement in the world) initiated the Religion Forum (R20) in conjunction with the Indonesian government where the group of

---

20. Pinnock, *Flame of Love*, 119.

21. Stott and Wright, *Christian Mission*, 131.

twenty of the most powerful economies around the world (G20) held their economic summit. This forum provides a platform for political leaders and religious thought leaders from around the world to enter into dialogue, with the goal of collaborating toward resolution of global problems.[22] As another example, in 2019 Pope Francis met with interreligious leaders in the United Arab Emirates and co-signed the Document on Human Fraternity for World Peace and Living Together, with the intention to foster collaboration among faiths to advance a culture of mutual respect.[23]

In a world that is constantly under religious tension and conflict, should Christians adopt a more conciliatory attitude in their encounters with individuals of other religions? As Christians interact with people of other faiths, it becomes imperative to understand the intricacies of this approach so that we can clarify our commitments in a globalized world. Because interreligious dialogue has taken on different meanings, understanding its objectives is important. Evangelicals differ from Catholics and mainline Protestants with regard to the various assumptions and attitudes they bring to dialogue, partly because of the implications already mentioned in terms of their goals in such encounters. As a result, many evangelicals have been hesitant to become involved in organized interreligious conversations, often viewing non-Christian religions as examples of human blindness, the direct work of Satan, or distortions of the truth that threaten the church's mission. Such attitudes have led to complete disengagement and withdrawal from these conversations. However, for productive dialogue to happen, the point of departure should not be the other person's particular religious adherence but their very "otherness," which should beckon us to come to the table to understand first and then seek to be understood.

22. Benthal, "The G20 Religion Forum."

23. Pope and Al-Tayyeb, "A Document."

Meaningful Approaches

But what exactly constitutes interreligious dialogue? Leonard Swidler describes dialogue as a "two-way communication" between individuals who hold differing views for the purpose of learning about the matter from one another.[24] Terry Muck offers a broad definition, affirming that "dialogue is an attempt to understand one another's faith traditions accurately."[25] Likewise, John Stott's general vision of dialogue is "an activity in its own right, whose goal is mutual understanding."[26] The Cape Town Commitment affirms the importance of bearing witness to the uniqueness of Christ as well as listening to others.[27] Broadly speaking, interreligious dialogue encompasses discussion between people who self-identify with a different religious tradition for the purpose of mutual understanding.

Furthermore, interreligious dialogue should be structured into levels of discussion to facilitate its practice. Jerald Gort proposes a fourfold structure for such an encounter. The first level is the *dialogue of histories*, in which a serious analysis of previous socio-political and economic relations between dialogical partners is properly conducted. Such dialogue acknowledges the painful injustices and misguided objections that people have executed against each other in the name of religion. The second tier is the *dialogue of theologies*, which aims to foster respect among people of various faiths while uncovering faulty assumptions that have been entertained due to a lack of knowledge. The third level is the *dialogue of spiritualities*, which includes sharing one's experiences of the sacred. Finally, there is the *dialogue of life*, which involves aspects of social concern where various faiths come together to collaborate on benevolent causes.[28]

24. Swidler, Duran, and Firestone, *Trialogue*, 7.

25. Muck, "Interreligious Dialogue," 188.

26. Stott, *Christian Mission*, 123.

27. Lausanne Movement, "Cape Town Commitment," III 1.e, 203.

28. Gort, "The Search," 758.

Terry Muck affirms that dialogue has an important place in missiological commitments. However, Muck suggests that dialogue is "only one of many possible ways of relating to people of other traditions."[29] Thus, he introduces five other modes of interaction that should be utilized when appropriate: pronouncement, argumentation, discussion, apologetics, and debate. The mode utilized would hinge on the cultural, religious, and social context in which the participants exist. Muck concludes by affirming that "a missional theology of dialogue. . .must be built on the capacity for human beings to have meaningful conversations with one another."[30] These are important considerations for constructing an evangelical approach to interreligious dialogue.

As another means of clarification, Harold Netland differentiates between formal and informal dialogue. The former consists of consultations in which participants of various religious traditions come together to pursue defined objectives, as in the case of R20 mentioned above. The latter occurs between two or more followers of different religions in unofficial settings. Netland argues that "informal dialogue is not only an option for evangelicals but is essential if the proclamation of the good news of salvation in Jesus Christ is to be carried out effectively."[31] There is no proclamation without proximity, and there is no proximity without dialogue.

Concluding Evaluation

A few evaluative remarks to bring this section to a proper closure are necessary. First, the tiers provided by Gort are helpful for structuring interreligious dialogue. An awareness of the history of interactions between groups is vital for interreligious dialogue to occur authentically. Toward this end, David Shenk notes that in light of the pain stored in a religious community's collective memory, extending and receiving mutual forgiveness are essential

29. Muck, "Interreligious Dialogue," 149.

30. Muck, "Interreligious Dialogue," 150.

31. Netland, *Dissonant Voices*, 296.

before honest conversation can occur. As a case in point, when Muslims were asked for ways to improve relations between the United States and Iran, the responses provided were summarized in one sentence: "Apologize for what you have done to us and respect us."[32] Apologizing for the mistakes and failures of the past may be the first step in building a suitable bridge to proclaiming the hope and transformative grace of Christ in a hostile world.

Second, engaging in informal dialogue can be a healthy sign of one's desire to break down barriers of animosity and ignorance while coming face to face with individuals who need the reconciliation that only Christ can offer. As Netland affirms, "Informal dialogue can be a demonstration of one's willingness to take the other person seriously as a fellow human being."[33] Properly carried out, dialogue should not be a stumbling block to evangelicals, but rather an opportunity to give witness to the power of the Spirit.

Third, Christians are called to the faithful exercise of theological reflection and dialogue in a constantly changing world where faith claims and religious traditions often clash. The fact that every human being has been created in God's image has serious implications for respecting and honoring others. When we affirm the stranger, we reaffirm the *imago Dei* imprinted in all of us. Affirming the religious other requires us to develop "an attitude of empathy, repentance, forgiveness, and willingness to be forgiven, even for the things for which we do not feel responsible."[34] We should develop a sense of love for dialogue driven by "many cups of tea—and the Holy Spirit."[35] Failing to understand the faith claims of other religions will prevent us from keeping up with the changing context of the modern world. As Tennent affirms, "Christianity is a faith for the world. It flourishes when challenged by unbelief, ridicule, and skepticism."[36] Ignoring the challenges inherent in our

32. Shenk, "Gospel," 8.

33. Netland, *Dissonant Voices,* 297.

34. Woodberry, "Terrorism," 6.

35. Shenk, "Gospel," 4.

36. Tennent, *Christianity,* 11.

changing context snuffs out opportunities for us to grow in our own faith.

Finally, it would be easier to remain isolated from other religious traditions, but this is a pathway to xenophobia. Therefore, we must actively reject preconceived notions about others that lead to unnecessary misunderstandings. As Terry Muck notes, "Dialogue cannot take place in a climate of hostility but only in a climate of love."[37] Although we are called to stand firm and "hold fast to the teachings passed on" to us (2 Thess 2:15), we must also stand in the gap on behalf of a globalized world that desperately needs the hope and peace offered only through the love of Jesus Christ. Ultimately, the *telos* of all theological and doctrinal discussions should be the glorification of God. In this sense, interreligious dialogue must become what Schroeder calls a "prophetic dialogue," requiring a "spirit of listening, learning, respect, and empathy [with] at the same time . . . honesty, conviction, faith, and courage to speak the truth as one knows it."[38] This kind of prophetic dialogue includes the art of listening and a commitment to provide a careful defense of one's faith.

37. Muck, "Interreligious Dialogue," 192.

38. Schroeder, "Proclamation," 57.

Part III

Ministering Holistically

6

Broken and Reconciled

Mission requires movement—first toward the Lord, then toward his Word, and finally toward the world. Central to the mission of God is the idea that life must be lived with an orientation toward others out of love for God. Humanity has an inherent longing for community and belonging—a place where one can be known and feel loved. The word *ubuntu* from the Zulu language, often translated as "I am because we are," may be a helpful concept to understand our inherent desire for community. Paul Ricoeur encapsulates this idea with the following words: "The selfhood of oneself implies otherness to such an intimate degree that one cannot be thought of without the other, that instead one passes into the other."[1] What is significant about Ricoeur's reflection is that through relationship with others we are able to discover ourselves more fully. But Ricoeur's affirmation that one cannot be thought of without the other seems somewhat surreal.

Community is essential to the survival and well-being of humanity, but undue emphasis on "togetherness" can be just as harmful as an unhealthy focus on the self. Life together does not mean a life encumbered or characterized by enmeshment. In fact, establishing healthy boundaries so that people do not "have to

---

1. Ricoeur, *Oneself,* 3.

separate"[2] is fundamental to healthy relationships. Differentiation is important to avoid falling into co-dependent patterns. Edwin Friedman puts it this way, "Differentiation refers to a direction in life rather than a state of being . . . differentiation is saying "I" when others are demanding "we." Differentiation is knowing where one ends and another begins."[3] The lack of self-differentiation proves to be just as problematic and harmful as the lack of community. Friedman suggests that individuals can be "self-ish" without being "selfish."[4] This means that despite our egocentric tendencies and ethnocentric attitudes, we should not dismiss the value of our self-hood nor the development of our personhood. Jesus was adamant that if we are to follow him, we must deny ourselves (Matt 16:24). He called us to deny that which is depriving us from living into our truest self, but not our whole self. Denying ourselves does not mean rejecting our personhood. On the contrary, it means that we bring our personhood to its fullest capacity by affirming what is intrinsically good in us and rejecting what has been marred by sinful tendencies and can continually damage us and our relationships.

The *Imago Dei*

Every person is a bearer of the image of God. An image is a representation of something or someone. When the biblical writers use the word "image" to describe who we are in relation to God, the word points to a resemblance, not in terms of a physical body, but rather the spiritual and moral likeness we have inherited from God. The moral quality of humanity was damaged by the fall and tarnished by sin. But in Jesus we see the image of God fully, for he is the exact "representation" of God's being and essence (Heb 1:3), and we will be restored into his image or likeness when our salvation is complete (Heb 2:6–15). Even when we might not bear the perfect image of God because of fragmentation in our soul, we

2. Friedman, *Failure*, 68.

3. Friedman, *Failure*, 183.

4. Friedman, *Failure*, 164.

retain the capacity to reflect something of God's divine essence—his love for one another.

The value inherent in human life itself in the eyes of God applies to all equally and without qualification. Al Tizon affirms, "The *Imago Dei*, intrinsic in the human person, not only makes life valuable; it also makes it sacred. As such, it deserves to be regarded with utmost dignity, respect, and protection."[5] God has endowed us with the capacity to love, grow, be fruitful, and live in relationship. This is what God had in view when he created man and woman in his image. Our human capacity to love and to hate, to injure and to heal, to defend and to offend is not based on isolated reasons or facts but is built on the bedrock of human interaction and our relationship with God. Regardless of how we view others, God views us in the same way, as objects of his mercy and targets of his love. David Gushee states, "No one can be excluded. From womb to womb, from home to far away, from friend to foe, all are covered. All must be viewed with reverence and treated with respect."[6]

Our life experiences have marred the core of our being and marked us in ways that seem contrary to God's original intention. Our brokenness has been largely affected by generational patterns and personal choices. But through an encounter with God's grace, God can redeem our past, heal our pain, and restore the honor he has always meant for us to carry on earth.

The Broken and Reconciled Self

Many unpredictable and unwarranted experiences in life can lead to a sense of defeat. Our self is fragile and easily wounded and threatened. Our individual reality connects us to the larger experience of the human race in which suffering and pain are a common experience to all. And yet we can step out of the painful past into a hopeful future as carriers of the grace and love that the Father offers to heal our wounds. Henri Nouwen, in his epic book

---

5. Tizon, *Whole and Reconciled*, 100.

6. Gushee, *Sacredness*, 388.

The Wounded Healer, explains: "In our own woundedness, we can become a source of life for others."[7] The journey towards healing happens through a process, with the help of the Holy Spirit and the support of others who become "wounded healers" to reconcile us back to God, ourselves, and each other.

If the broken self is a microcosm of a broken world, we can conclude that both the self and the world await its full reconciliation and complete restoration, and what is possible today is only a foretaste of what will be a complete reality one day. The Hebrew word *shalom* paints this picture as it points to the type of wholeness, justice, well-being, and fullness of life that every creature longs to enjoy—all of which leads to a holistic sense of peace. *Shalom* embodies a complex biblical concept that reflects the very nature of God and his will for creation.[8] Prior to extending the peace of God to others, we must first make peace with ourselves. As Al Tizon explains, "Before we participate with God in 'saving the world' (that is, engaging in the ministry of reconciliation), we look upward to God to heal and reconcile the broken pieces of our interior selves."[9] In this process, Tizon continues to affirm that reconciliation and restoration involve four steps: the vertical, between us and God; the internal, within ourselves; the horizontal, between us and others; and the external, between us and the cosmos. To the extent that we work toward the experience of reconciliation with all these interrelated aspects of life, we move toward restoring the dignity of the self.[10]

The journey toward reconciliation begins with a journey inward, allowing God to heal the center of our being, reveal our inclinations, and dissect our thoughts so that we may become able to serve him from a position of humility. This maturity requires us to be attentive to the rhythms of self-care. To be missionally minded and present in the margins, where brokenness and scarcity abound, we must pay attention to the ongoing needs of our own self. Our

---

7. Nouwen, *Wounded Healer*, 28.

8. Tizon, *Whole and Reconciled*, 85.

9. Tizon, *Whole and Reconciled*, 103.

10. Tizon, *Whole and Reconciled*, 103.

well-being is of utmost importance in the extension of God's purposes and plans. Therefore, careful and intentional consideration must be given to holistic care for our human existence—the physical, psycho-emotional, relational, and spiritual—so that we can be duly equipped and prepared to serve others. Paying careful attention to nutrition, exercise, therapy, accountability, social relationships, spiritual practices, and education brings the self into balance and restores homeostasis within us.

The process toward reconciliation begins with a look inward but cannot stop at introspection; it must move upward to the God who reconciles us back to himself. The biblical concept and ideal of the reconciliation of all things is both God's hope *in us* and promise *to us*. God invites us into a rich fellowship with him so that we may move toward horizontal reconciliation. In other words, being reconciled to God is not enough to make us ambassadors of reconciliation in the world. We must also move outward and be reconciled to our brothers and sisters along the lines that have kept us apart, recognizing that sometimes these efforts cannot be carried out in their fullness because reconciliation takes work. Sometimes full reconciliation is not possible, but simply because one party is unwilling to engage in the process, the other party should not shy away from its duty to at least attempt it. Nevertheless, God is the one who sets in motion such a process, and he will bring it to completion one day. As Miroslav Volf says, we should not be focused on "how to achieve the final reconciliation," but on the "resources we need to live in the absence of final reconciliation."[11] That is, God's ongoing project of reconciliation requires us to acquire the necessary skills and practices that will allow us to move toward full reconciliation one day.

The Reconciled Community

The call to be reconciled in a community must follow a similar trajectory. It must turn toward the ecclesial community in which

11. Volf, *Exclusion and Embrace*, 89.

it finds itself and then outward to other communities. The community of faith must first be reconciled to itself before it can become ambassadors of reconciliation in the world. The church is divided along many lines. How can we expect a broken world to know the power of the risen Christ and sanctifying Spirit when our life together has become strained? Reconciliation is the bedrock of *shalom* and involves repairing social ties, especially within the Christian community.

God reconciled us to himself through Christ, who eliminated the barriers of sin that once separated us from God. The blood of Christ also brought those who were far away near, breaking the walls of hostility and the barriers that once separated us from each other in order to create a new humanity (Eph 2:13). Christ himself is our peace (Eph 2:14), he came and preached peace (Eph 2:17), and he made peace on our behalf to reconcile us to God (Eph 2:15–16). Peacemaking is not the same as peacekeeping. Peacemaking leads to peace building whereas peacekeeping sometimes hinders true peace. Granted, peacekeeping may be a useful temporary recourse at times when conflict is high. Nevertheless, peacekeeping shies away from the continual effort needed to reconcile perspectives, resolve conflict, and address solutions, as its focus is on keeping people away from each other as a way to prevent further damage or dissension. It simply "keeps" things at bay while "keeping" people apart. Peacemaking, on the other hand, is the process of forging a resolution between the disagreeing or disputing parties to help them work together toward mutual understanding. Peacemaking is possible only when we move toward conflict and embrace it rather than escape it, but to attain this ideal one must address the source of the conflict and be ready to offer an apology when necessary as well as extend forgiveness.

Jesus is the mediator between the Father and his children. He knows our pain, so he is able to mediate God's grace to us. He understands our brokenness, so he reflects God's love for us. To be reconciled with each other means letting go of past hurts. Because this takes time and forgiveness is a process, reconciliation is not magical or mechanical. It is sacred. The reconciled people of God reflect the essence of God's nature to a world that is constantly breaking and bleeding. In the reconciled community of the church, God carries on his mission more visibly and vividly as the church operates as a conduit of grace into a broken world.

The holistic essence of God's redemptive purposes includes the extension of *shalom* into every corner of the earth. Disciples who focus only on enjoying peace with God but fail to extend the peace of God to others forsake their missional calling. God calls us to be peacemakers in a world of hate lovers. Because God's primary concern is for the holiness, wholeness, and restoration of his creation, his own holiness, his love for his creation, and his wrath toward sin are inseparable. His love and wrath, as well as his glory and righteousness, constitute his holiness. And it is his holiness that sets him apart. God's holiness is freedom from all evil and sin, because God is light and in him there is no darkness (1 John 1:5). His divine character is understood as a combination of his thoughts, fellowship within the Trinity, and actions that cohere with each other. Jesus' command to be perfect as the Father is perfect (Matt 5:48) is a call to abide in him and, consequently, to love others through his love. This love is not a sentimental, emotional, or temporary feeling toward the object of our affection. On the contrary, it is a self-giving, self-abandoning, and self-emptying kind of love that lends itself to a much larger project: *shalom*. Against this backdrop, we can see mission as both a contributor to spiritual growth and an indicator of spiritual vitality in the journey toward becoming ambassadors of reconciliation in the world.

The entire church of Jesus Christ must be a prophetic presence in society and must model the power of the gospel to bring restoration and reconciliation across racial, cultural, and religious lines. As Al Tizon points out, "To the extent that the church makes good on this opportunity to be the whole global church from the margins, it positions itself to become an agent of reconciliation that its Lord has called it to be in a fractured world."[12] The church is endowed with strength and purpose from the God who reigns above, below, and beyond our comprehension. Therefore, we are

12. Tizon, *Whole and Reconciled,* 31.

recipients and channels of grace as we participate in the mission of God in a diverse and fractured world.

Living for the Sake of the World

A spirituality destitute of a life of service and a heart of compassion, seeking only to protect itself from the possible perils of the world, will likely wither, crumble, and die in the valley of self-preservation. Through a vibrant, ongoing relationship with God, we become infused with the capability to help others find such a relationship as well. Rejecting a self-focused search for fulfillment and embarking on a self-giving journey will, paradoxically, lead one to find his or her truest self in Christ. When we walk in the power and freedom of our truest selves, we become compelled to love and serve one another. A vital spirituality cannot be divorced from missional living. Accordingly, Susan Muto wrote, "Christian spirituality and Christian mission are two sides of the same coin."[13] The more we grow into the likeness of Christ, the more the world will see Christ in us.

In John 21:15–17, we find a clear example of the important place that a missional act holds in the life of believers. In this passage, Jesus reinstates Peter and calls him to return to the redemptive partnership Jesus initiated. The posture that Jesus wants Peter to embrace in this instance is not one of surrender nor repentance, but of service. In other words, Peter's redemption is evidenced through his willingness to serve and feed the people for whom Jesus died. Jesus uses the Greek word *boskō* (translated as *feed* in the NIV) twice in this passage to imply the action required of Peter in demonstration of his love for Jesus. The "feeding" Peter is called to do is not literal but symbolic. Jesus calls Peter to serve others as an indication that he has surrendered to the ways of Jesus and confessed him as Lord. The feeding involves service to others, which is one of the meanings that the Greek word *boskō* renders.[14]

13. Muto, "Living Contemplatively," 82.

14. BDAG 181.

Likewise, by feeding a lost world with the living Word, we will give evidence of our love for God.

True spirituality cannot be divorced from a life of service. Dwight Zscheile affirms, "Spiritual formation is not just for our own individual growth; it is for love of God and neighbor."[15] Thus, by virtue of its nature, the path of spirituality must be marked by social holiness. Robert Mulholland recognizes the link between a spirituality embedded in the community of faith and communal social concern when he states, "Corporate spirituality and social spirituality are inseparable elements of the wholeness of our journey in faith."[16] He further states, "Holistic spirituality is a pilgrimage of deepening responsiveness to God's control of our life and being."[17] Thus, a holistic spirituality that incorporates individual communion with God and corporate worship must transfer its energies into holistic ministry and service to others in different contexts and particular situations.

Doxological Mission

The church's mission on earth begins and culminates with doxology. In its praise, adoration, and worship, the church is both blessed and empowered to become restored and restorative in the presence of the King and in the presence of others. Living doxologically allows us to set our eyes on the One who gave his life for those in the world, because adoration humbles us. The name of Jesus is above every other name; therefore, he is worthy to receive all praise.

Living doxologically when the winds of life are in our favor seems a lot easier than when the winds are against us. Perhaps one of the most trying aspects of the Christian life is to live missionally in times when pain and suffering overwhelm us. How do we praise God and thank him when tragedy hits unexpectedly? How

15. Zscheile, "Missional Theology," 8.

16. Mulholland, *Invitation to a Journey,* 193.

17. Mulholland, *Invitation to a Journey,* 193.

do we worship our Father when he seems absent in light of our experience with evil and pain? We cannot make sense of reality at times, and that conception blurs our perception of God's reality. The problem of suffering has often been treated in theological studies under the lens of theodicy to provide a rationale for the existence of evil in light of the goodness of God. Walter Brueggemann observes, "Any 'world' that is 'made' in liturgy which does not include honest elements of pain is a false world that leads to death."[18] Therefore, something more than human reason must be employed to help us direct our gaze from our suffering onto its redemptive purpose. David Duke has suggested, "Suffering needs to be given voice in worship to help hurting people move from despair and silent passivity to hope-filled, courageous action."[19] Worship is both the duty and the delight of the human community, which highlights the power of praise as expressed through tears, sighs, prayer, silence, singing, and lamenting. There is weeping, but there is also rejoicing. There is mourning, but also the hope of a new morning. Brueggemann captures this dialectic approach: "Mourning is a precondition in another way. It is not a formal, external requirement but rather the only door and route to joy."[20]

Worship is often conceived as a practice of giving thanks for all that God has *done*, and it certainly is, but we often overlook the place of lament as a way to express what we think God seems to have left *undone*. In the Psalms, we find a collection of prayers and hymns that reveal the value of wailing and sobbing while remembering God's sovereignty, faithfulness, and providence. The Psalmists give voice to their delight and doubt in God. The prayers of lament so passionately articulated in the Psalms show us how to express ourselves before God when we have doubts and question his goodness or his ability to rescue us. When the tides and stormy gales seem to have left us depleted and confused, lament helps us empty our soul of the sorrow that overburdens it. Lament serves as a cathartic expression and pathway to liberate our

18. Brueggemann, *Israel's Praise*, 133.

19. Duke, "Giving Voice to Suffering," 263.

20. Brueggemann, *Israel's Praise*, 132.

innermost pain through tears and sighs. Prayers of lament are also "opportunities for honest encounters with God in solidarity with the faith community."[21] The process of wailing and grieving does not eradicate our pain; it simply lessens its burdensome weight. As Brueggemann says, "Access to life is mostly through the resistant door of pain."[22] Walking through our pain allows us to give voice to anguish so we may release our anger and fears and find relief and understanding instead.

In times of suffering, lament allows us to confront our pain and find consolation in our pain. When we muster the strength to confront our own inadequacy and inability to fix ourselves, we become more realistic about the fact that only God's presence can bring us true consolation. By inviting the community of faith to pray for those who face adversity, we exemplify more clearly what it means to be a doxological community. This doxological practice allows us to be witnesses to God's boundless grace and to see his rescuing power as a "foretaste of the coming victory of God's mission."[23] Worship in the mission of God is not only to bring glory to God but also to lead us to the experience of holiness. Worship is not instrumental, but transformational. Through worship, Christians exalt God. As Job declared in the crucible of his pain, "The Lord gave and the Lord has taken away; may the name of the Lord be praised" (Job 1:21). The very faithfulness of God beckons us to come and respond to his grace even when we might not fully understand his ways.

Furthermore, it is not only in lament and mourning that we find a way to express our worship, but also through gratitude. As Henri Nouwen so beautifully expresses, "Gratitude in its deepest sense means to live life as a gift to be received thankfully. True gratitude embraces all of life: the good and the bad, the joyful and the painful, the holy and the not-so-holy. We do this because we become aware of God's presence in the middle of all that

21. Brueggemann, *Israel's Praise*, 133.

22. Brueggemann, *Israel's Praise*, 133.

23. Flemming, *Recovering the Full Mission*, 245.

happens."[24] Being grateful requires us to look beyond our present circumstances and sing about the victory of a crucified and risen Lord, anticipating the final triumph of the Kingdom of our Lord.

The capacity to see our reality through different lenses is like developing a "double vision," to borrow a phrase by Thomas Nagel, who calls us to see the world "from nowhere" as well as "from here."[25] This double vision has nothing to do with the simultaneous perception of two images that overlap each other when one focuses on an object. Rather, it reveals the possibility of seeing things from two different vantage points.[26] Following Nagel's conceptualization, I would add that rather than seeing the world "from nowhere" and "from here," we must learn to see our world "from the present" and "from the future." That is, while the world in its present condition is fragmented and fractured, we must remember that God is making all things new and one day his creation will be completely healed and restored.

Biblical scholar Mitchell Reddish says it well: "We are a community that sees the world differently from the way others see it. Where others see brokenness, we see wholeness. Where others see death, we see love. Where others see a world in rebellion, we see a world transformed. . . confident that the love and mercy of God will ultimately bring healing to a fractured world."[27] We may live in a world of brokenness, death, and rebellion. We should neither be oblivious nor blinded to these realities. Nevertheless, in the midst of brokenness, death, and rebellion we are reminded that these are temporary conditions and that God wants to use us to bring about the restoration of all things through his mercy and love.

24. Nouwen, *Turn my Mourning*, 17.

25. Nagel, *The View from Nowhere*, 62.

26. Nagel, *The View from Nowhere*, 63.

27. Reddish, *Revelation*, 225.

7

To the Ends of the Earth

AMONG THE SITUATIONS IN life that often intertwine the reality of loss with the prospect of new life is the experience of migration. In recent decades, the topic of immigration has fostered polemical disputes that have left society frightened and unable to respond adequately. This situation demands missiological reflection to help the church navigate these turbulent times through hospitable practices. While some theologians have focused on formulating an ethics of place and solidarity toward the dispossessed,[1] others have offered a careful analysis of the conditions immigrants experience, seeking to raise awareness of the inconsistencies in poorly framed immigration policies.[2] This topic has received its fair share of evaluation from a myriad of angles and perspectives, but the present chapter highlights the marvelous opportunities we now have available to reach the nations through mass migration all over the world.

1. See Payne, *Strangers Next Door*; Prill, *Global Mission on Our Doorstep*.

2. See Sorens and Hwang, *Welcoming the Stranger*; De la Torre, *The U.S. Immigration Crisis*.

Biblical Principles

Global movements of people have taken place since the beginning of time, and the sovereign Lord has used them to further his Kingdom in fruitful ways, even when the course of these movements has not resulted in recognizably hopeful outcomes. Biblical stories narrate in detail the geographic movement of our spiritual forefathers as they followed the will of God by faith. Abraham and Sarah set out to live in an unknown land. Joseph, his brothers, and their children lived as slaves in Egypt. Moses and the Israelites transited through the wilderness in search of the Promised Land. The experience of the exiles in Babylon became a source of loss as well as a time of reflection. Ruth and Naomi relocated to Naomi's land in search of a better life. The prophets lived in foreign lands, enduring periods of great suffering and pain. Jesus journeyed through arduous places. The apostles and the newly formed Christian communities attempted to live out the gospel in a context that was often hostile to them. All these examples point to the frequent necessity of immigration, under favorable or unfavorable circumstances, whether forced or voluntary, permanent or transitory.[3]

The biblical narratives address the stories of immigrants from a social and ethical standpoint as they describe the relationship of the people of God to their neighbors and the moral responsibility of Israel toward foreigners residing in their land. The Scriptures make it quite evident that God expected Israel to be hospitable to sojourners and strangers. One of the abiding and guiding mandates God set forth for his people stated, "The strangers who sojourn with you shall be to you as the natives among you, and you shall love them as yourself; for you were strangers in the land of Egypt" (Lev 19:33). Israel's ethical obligation to love the sojourner rested on the fact that they had been sojourners themselves and that God had made provision for them to break free from the cruel conditions they had experienced, as well as taking them to a better place. Loving the sojourner is a clear mandate for the follower of Christ as well. One of the ethical implications of love is to "practice

3. Campese, "The Irruption of Migrants," 3.

hospitality" (Rom 12:13). The word translated "hospitality" is the Greek *philoxenia*, which literally means "love of strangers."[4]

God's love for the stranger is such a predominant theme in the Scriptures that God became incarnated as an alien. The most radical feature of the incarnation is not just that God came to the earth to become one of us, but that he came as one who was vulnerable and homeless—an immigrant and stranger. Jesus and his family journeyed in Egypt as political refugees and undocumented migrants, fleeing Herod's tyrannical rule and heavy hand of oppression. Following Herod's death, Joseph, Mary, and Jesus migrated to Nazareth, where Jesus grew up and began his ministry until the time when he set his face toward Jerusalem, where he died outside the city gate.

After Jesus' death and resurrection and not long after the church was formed, a great persecution ensued against the church in Jerusalem, and the disciples scattered throughout Judea and Samaria. Although this unpredictable circumstance forced many of the disciples to flee and endure imprisonment, the resulting diffusion of the believers also produced unprecedented opportunities to advance the gospel, fulfilling the promise of Jesus (Acts 1:8). The dispersion of believers throughout these regions culminated in a church being planted in Samaria and the gospel spreading to North Africa. As believers migrated into Phoenicia, Cyprus, and Antioch (Acts 11:19), a relatively large church formed in Antioch, where believers were called Christians for the first time (Acts 11:26). The connection between forced migrations and global evangelization is strikingly clear through the experience of the Jewish diaspora. As difficult as it was for the disciples to leave their home, their sacrifice resulted in the multiplication of churches and the advancement of the gospel in other regions. The gospel began to transform communities and reached other ethnic groups, such as the Samaritans and Greeks.

But the people of God who migrated did not always do so under compulsion. In other instances, the people of God migrated voluntarily, leaving their places of comfort to obey God,

4. BDAG 684.

recognizing that they were citizens of a better kingdom. The people of God as sojourners on earth, on transit and just passing through, are pilgrims on a mission. In the meantime, our mission is especially to the margins—that is, to reaching the least of these, the lost, and the last with the liberating news of the gospel.

Diaspora Missiology

The church *on mission* is to and through people *on the move.* The number of displaced peoples and refugees keeps increasing, spurring people to seek refuge in stable communities. The search for better living conditions has driven people around the world to escape the harsh realities of extremism, war, and poverty that have plagued them. As ethnic groups begin to gather in different communities around the world, they form what is known as diaspora communities. "Diaspora" refers to people who have left their countries and are now scattered and dispersed around the world. Diaspora missiology is a "framework for understanding and participating in God's redemptive mission among peoples living outside their places of origin."[5] Both the Old and New Testaments use the term "diaspora" to refer to the Jews living outside Israel. In the New Testament, the term refers in particular to those who were forced out of their land due to persecution and were forced to scatter throughout surrounding areas.

In recent decades, diaspora missiology has been at the forefront of research studies, especially in light of the ongoing refugee crises around the world and the unprecedented number of people on the move.[6] Much of the focus of contemporary diaspora missiology has centered on missionary efforts to the diaspora. Enoch Wan identifies three types of diaspora missions: missions aimed at reaching members of the diaspora, missions through diaspora Christians to reach their own people wherever they are, and

5. Tira and Yamamori, *Scattered and Gathered,* 7.

6. For a sampling, see Pocock and Wan (eds.), *Diaspora Missiology*; Tira and Yamamori (eds.), *Gathered and Scattered*; Wan, *Diaspora Missiology: Theory, Methodology and Practice*; and George and Adeney, *Refugee Diaspora.*

missions beyond the diaspora, which mobilize diaspora Christians for cross-cultural missions to other ethnic or racial groups other than their own.[7]

Entering a host country presents many challenges. Every refugee, migrant worker, or residency seeker faces a variety of needs, such as language acquisition, finding employment, and schooling for their children. Migrants face complex situations—physical vulnerability, psychological trauma, issues of self-identity, lack of legal protection, and other conditions. All forms of human displacement create complexities as to how individuals affected by these transitions navigate life, relationships, identity, and cultural change. It is not uncommon for individuals living in the diaspora to encounter difficulties in their host country. Robin Cohen reflects, "There is barely a group that did not at some stage experience discrimination in the countries to which they migrated."[8] Though the attitude and effects of discrimination seem unavoidable at times, groups in the diaspora can form a unique diasporic identity, leading to positive results, including the formation of creative and enriching spaces where virtues may be learned and dangers and trauma escaped.[9]

A plethora of nonprofit organizations, Christian and secular alike, have sought to welcome refugees and help with the legal needs of immigrants. An example of a secular organization is Exodus Refugee, located in Indianapolis, which provides basic necessities, community resources, mental health counseling, classes in English as a second language (ESL), school supplies, and employment search assistance.[10] An example of a Christian-based organization is Exodus World Service, located near Chicago, seeking to mobilize the Christian community by educating churches about the plight immigrants face and equipping the church to welcome and befriend refugees.[11] Partnering with

7. Wan, *Diaspora Missiology*, 5.

8. Cohen, *Global Diasporas*, 7.

9. Cohen, *Global Diasporas*, 8.

10. See https://www.exodusrefugee.org

11. See https://www.exodusworldservice.org

such organizations is a wonderful way to minister to the needs of refugees and immigrants.

In our world today, people are on the move, from the margins into the margins, but God is also on the move, from his throne into the obscurity of society so that the gospel may be known in every corner of our world. Sam George and Miriam Adeney assert, "Mission in the margins always emerges in unclear forms, but it is characterized by clear signs of advancement of the gospel, empowerment by the Holy Spirit, and—as a result—changes to the very nature of Christian faith and our conceptions of it."[12] It is against this backdrop that we capture the vision of ministry in the margins *to* and *with* people on the move.

Diaspora mission depends on the intentional and practical participation of the local church as it recognizes the work, the privilege, and the responsibility to which we are called in caring for the stranger. Global nomads might be more open to the gospel than at home, where persecution, family pressure, and government restrictions limit them in significant ways. With the religious freedom available in the West, the church has an opportunity to minister to the diasporic community.

Reaching the Least Reached

One crucial priority of missions should be to reach individuals from areas that have had little contact with the gospel message. According to the *Joshua Project,* a ministry of Frontier Ventures that provides statistical analysis of the progress of the gospel around the world, approximately 17,446 people groups exist in the world, and more than 7,400 of them are considered unreached.[13] The Global Research department of the International Mission Board also provides reliable data on how to engage unreached people groups around the world. An unreached people group (UPG) is a "people group among which there is no indigenous community

12. George and Adeney, *Refugee Diaspora,* xxi.

13. See https://www.joshuaproject.net

of believing Christians with adequate numbers and resources to evangelize the rest of its members without outside (cross-cultural) assistance."[14] A similar concept is the notion of "Unengaged Unreached People Groups" (UUPGs) who do not have a church planting strategy in their midst. Global Research estimates that there are currently 3,177 UUPGs around the world.[15]

The notion of UPGs was first formulated by missiologists to express the necessity of advancing strategies to finish the task of missions. Since its early conceptualization, the term has been used to indicate the common history, language, beliefs, and identity shared by a particular ethnic group of people. Early missiologists, such as Ralph Winter and Bruce Koch, utilized the concept of UPGs to measure progress toward completing the task of reaching the world with the gospel message.[16] However, recent missiologists have challenged the premises of this concept, spurring missiologists to move beyond it in theory and practice.[17] Lee and Park argue that many mission strategies represent a "normative application of the homogeneous unit principle (HUP) to cross-cultural mission, which results in a failure to take seriously biblical mandates for Christian reconciliation and unity in diversity."[18] They advocate for a missiology that is intentional in creating multicultural communities instead of reaching out only to particular ethnic groups. Nevertheless, focusing on evangelizing UPGs is not necessarily contrary to creating multicultural communities.

Whether the concept will continue to be utilized in the future or fade away over time, completing the task of world evangelization by maximizing opportunities to present the gospel to all peoples should remain at the forefront of our agenda. With the rapid flow of immigrants from places that have had little access to the gospel, the opportunity to reach UPGs in their new homeland is more viable. Most of these groups flock to urban centers. For example,

14. Johnstone, *People Groups*, 37.

15. For further information, see https://www.peoplegroups.org

16. Winter and Koch, *Advancing the Task*, 16.

17. Lee and Park, *Beyond People Group Thinking*, 212.

18. Lee and Park, *Beyond People Group Thinking*, 213–14.

in New York City alone, 48 different UPGs have been reported.[19] Organizations dedicated to ministering to and caring for refugees, immigrants, and UPGs in North America have embraced this task. For instance, Global Gates is an evangelical mission organization committed to mobilizing prayer and missionaries for the purpose of ministry to UPGs.

Many individuals from UPGs who have migrated to gateway cities have the opportunity to come in contact with Christians. Global Gates, for example, offers opportunities for short-term mission trips to gateway cities, such as San Francisco, Washington, D.C., and New York, with the intention of engaging in conversation with unreached people, hearing their stories, offering prayer and hospitality through various means. This organization has identified and mapped out several ways to be missional among various groups. It distributes language-specific materials and encourages team members to be present in the community, such as by eating at local restaurants and befriending individuals in their workplaces. Fulfilling the call to spread the gospel across ethnic lines and cultural barriers is now more possible than ever and can be done in our backyard.

Priority must be given to further research to help organizations develop strategies for outreach ministries to unevangelized people groups. Most foreigners residing in the United States, however, do not come from unreached people groups but from lands that are centers of Christian vitality. With the continual flow of immigrants to the West, and particularly to the United States, it is also imperative to understand how to relate to, integrate, and learn from the immigrant church. Being hospitable to Christian immigrants is another way to move toward Christian reconciliation. In view of the opportunities ethnic communities can offer the American church to become more missionally minded, it is extremely important to consider how to partner with ethnic churches in our neighborhood so that resources can flow into effective outreach.

19. Global Gates, "Gateway City."

Reversing the Flow of Missions

Christianity was still primarily a Western religion at the beginning of the 20th century. By the end of the century, however, the majority of Christians were concentrated outside the Western world. Areas that once were the mission field have now become the missionary force. These new centers of Christian vitality have created a multidirectional, polycentric mission, exerting a "dramatic influence on the whole missionary enterprise."[20] As non-Western nations participate in and initiate mission endeavors around the world, a phenomenon known as "reverse missions" has appeared. Hun Kim asserts that reverse mission takes place "when non-Western churches return with the Gospel to societies that initially brought the Gospel to them."[21] Reverse missionaries exhibit a profound sense of duty in sharing the gospel with diasporic immigrants as well as seeking to revitalize the secular West.

In the new global Christian paradigm, this phenomenon has favorable prospects. People from countries that were traditionally the receivers of missionary endeavors have now been sent to work in countries that were once the senders. The reverse flow began initially as a response to the discontent felt by non-Western indigenous leaders who felt that the direction of missionary efforts had been unilateral. Later, it turned into an opportunity to participate in the missionary mandate around the world. Although most of the scholarly discussion of reverse mission has centered on African-led churches in the West,[22] a few scholars have also considered Latin American reverse missionary efforts[23] while others describe the impact of the Asian ethnic churches planted in neighborhoods in Western countries.[24] In some cases, Global South missionaries are attempting to re-evangelize the secular West by ministering to

20. Tennent, *Invitation*, 31.
21. Kim, "Receiving Mission," 63.
22. See Ajani, "Migration and Mission."
23. See Cueva, *Mission Partnership*.
24. Rah, *Next Evangelicalism*, 165–66.

the dominant group,[25] but most seem to minister specifically to their own ethnic group in the diaspora.[26]

In the context of the United States, American sociologist Robert Wuthnow believes that the scope of the reverse mission movement should not be "exaggerated," as the tens of thousands of foreign missionaries "said to be working in the United States could well describe nothing more than immigrant pastors ministering to immigrant congregations."[27] Another variation on the practice is Reverse Short-Term Missions (RSTM),[28] where individuals from the Majority World go on a mission trip with the intention of fostering relationships with their host. This effort can invigorate individuals in Western congregations who otherwise would not come in contact with Christians from other parts of the world, and it can stimulate fervor for evangelism and missions in churches that are stagnant or dormant. It remains uncertain whether reverse mission efforts will concentrate largely on compatriots in the diaspora or if they will be part of a strategic plan by churches in the Global South to re-evangelize the West. Either way, the opportunities for the advancement of the kingdom of God are promising.

The Beauty of Hospitality

In a world of global movements, hospitality is crucial to the credibility of the gospel. People tend to come to faith because they have seen and experienced the love of God through a hospitable community. Hospitality has become a buzzword often equated with tolerance. But true hospitality is a life-giving practice based on biblical concepts that invite us to see others in like manner as we should view ourselves—as pilgrims on a journey, sojourners passing through, and aliens in this world. Our own sense of displacement is important to help us welcome strangers who need a

25. Asamoha-Gyadu, "African Pentecostal," 297.

26. Adedibu, "Reverse Mission," 406.

27. Wuthnow, *Boundless Faith*, 56.

28. Twibell, "Reversing the Flow," 3.

place to belong, for our citizenship is first and foremost a heavenly one. Surely, we are rooted in culture and so are our churches, but our identity should always be formed by the values of the kingdom of God. Hostile environments create many difficulties in navigating the practice of hospitality, but seeing ourselves as displaced individuals who are also on a journey to our real home might help to create sensitivity to the needs of others on their present journey.

When a person is introduced and welcomed into the Christian community, that individual embarks on a journey toward their real home. In their mission to reach our surrounding contexts, Christians must choose to embrace what Miroslav Volf calls a "soft difference"—a posture that is strong yet kind in our witness.[29] Volf affirms, "For people who live the soft difference, mission fundamentally takes the form of witness and invitation."[30] Witness and invitation are the pillars of hospitality. There is no true hospitality without understanding our loyalty to the King who reigns in the heavenly city. Our witness becomes more vividly expressed when we remember whom we are representing and make a genuine effort to invite others into the same journey.

The Church as a Community of Hosts

True hospitality begins with prayer. The biblical command to care for others requires action, but as Christians, our first step of action must be prayer. Through prayer, we can bear each other's burdens as we lift them to our Father and trust that he will move on our behalf. And it is in prayer that we listen to the voice of the Spirit as he guides us to extend his grace to those who might have no place to call home. We can also pray for policies and laws to reflect the type of justice that God desires for us and for the well-being of our cities. Moreover, in prayer we are reminded that we cannot do anything apart from the Father, and that he alone does all things through us. As Henri Nouwen has stated, "A growing intimacy

29. Volf, "Soft Difference," 24.

30. Volf, "Soft Difference," 24.

with God deepens our sense of responsibility for others. It evokes in us an always increasing desire to bring the whole world with all its suffering and pains around the divine fire in our heart and to share the revitalizing heat with all who want to come."[31] When we are on our knees, we humbly display the posture of a heart fully surrendered to loving others as God has loved us.

Hospitality also involves redirecting our gaze toward those who are forced out of their lands and displaced for reasons outside their control. Most individuals are simply waiting for people to invite them into their lives, and our witness is greatly diminished if the walls we have unknowingly built in the hidden corners of our mind keep us away from the very people we are called to love. Henri Nouwen, once again, describes our opportunity to displace ourselves by reaching out to the displaced: "The paradox of voluntary displacement is that although it seems to separate us from the world . . . we actually find ourselves in deeper union with it."[32] Through voluntary displacement into communities that have been displaced involuntarily, we demonstrate the basic principles of the Christian faith. Christ has welcomed us and continually invites us to drink from the fountain of God's grace so as to quench both our thirst and that of a broken world, because hospitality is the heart of the Christian faith.

Guests and Hosts

The beauty of hospitality is carried out in recognition of the loving hospitality that Jesus has extended to us. He is a host, but he is also a guest. Being a guest without a proper welcome can be unsettling and detrimental. But we can take comfort, should we ever find ourselves in that position, in the fact that Jesus has been there too. Being a guest entails taking a vulnerable and dependent position, one that resembles the attitude Jesus desires of us and modeled for us. He came to his own, and his own did not recognize him (John

31. Nouwen, *Compassion,* 109.

32. Nouwen, *Compassion,* 64.

1:1); he was initially welcomed by his people only to be rejected and pushed to the outskirts of the city (Luke 4:16–30); he was defamed and labeled a lunatic (Mark 3:21); but he chose to call himself a stranger in his identification with the hurting (Matt 25:35). Jesus made himself a guest on purpose at times, such as when he invited himself to the house of Zacchaeus (Luke 19:1–10); he was a guest in other people's homes, such as at the home of Simon the Leper (Luke 7:36; Matt 26:6) or when Martha welcomed him in and prepared a meal for him (Luke 10:38); and he was a guest without honor when he visited temples and synagogues, especially in his hometown.

In his function as a host, Jesus gathered people, little ones found comfort in his arms, masses listened to him while they were fed, the broken were healed, and individuals considered impure by the religious crowds were restored. But Jesus was a strange host as he did not even claim to have a place to lay his head (Matt 8:20). To choose to be a stranger is to take a subservient role, but it also offers others a congenial opportunity to practice true hospitality. As Anthony Gittins observes, "As people who cross boundaries and enter other worlds, we have no business to claim the role of host or one up, and every reason to acquiesce in our role as guest/stranger or one down."[33] In taking up the role of guests or strangers, we also learn how to be better hosts. This dual interaction shows the binary role of human relationships, where at times we might be the guest and at other times we are hosts.

The practice of hospitality is a means by which we position ourselves as ambassadors of the kingdom of God. It is a practice built on giving and receiving. One of the best resources that communities possess is their willingness to share fellowship and friendship with others. Beyond just offering a service or reception to people, we must welcome people into our lives and way of living. Hospitable communities become fully alive when they provide a space for people to be heard and feel valued. Although boundaries are often places of obstruction, they can also become places of construction. We can rest assured that God has been

33. Gittins, *Ministry at the Margins*, 148.

at these junctures all along, rebuilding a community to welcome those whom Jesus has always embraced.

Mission, by its very nature, implies crossing boundaries and breaking barriers. To recover its identity, the church must break through lines of division and disengagement to make the boundaries penetrable and porous, and a sacred space for a mutual encounter. Many individuals living in the margins have been forced to live there. Others have opted to be with people in the margins. The church has the opportunity to choose to be fully immersed and present with all those who have been forced to be there far longer. John Driver comments, "When mission flows from centers of power and prestige, a certain kind of gospel is communicated, different from when the gospel is shared in weakness from its social periphery."[34] The church can recover its authenticity only through an honest acknowledgement of its weakness and powerlessness, occupying a position of vulnerability and dependence.

34. Driver, *Images*, 227.

8

Caring for the Poor

OUR WORLD IS IN a continual state of need. The Bible describes how poverty has affected the world and how the church can serve as a means of healing and assistance for people living in poverty. This responsibility does not belong to the church exclusively, however. The Scriptures are clear that everyone should care for the poor: individuals (Matt 25:31–46), families (1 Tim 5:8), as well as governments (Dan 4:27). To add to the list, in the contemporary world, many nonprofit organizations and parachurch ministries have undertaken efforts aimed at alleviating poverty as well.

When we consider the role that the church plays in this daunting task, we have to recognize that it is rooted in the very works of Jesus. Just as Jesus preached the good news of the Kingdom through word and deed, the church is called to acquire tools and skills to share resources contextually. Because Jesus came to preach the good news to the poor (Luke 4:18), we are also invited to follow him into the places of brokenness and fragmentation around the world to serve and care for the poor. The tasks of the church should mirror the ministry of Jesus, who fed the hungry, clothed the naked, visited the prisoner, healed the sick, and set up principles for peacemaking so we may work for the welfare of our cities.

John Wesley's sermons inspire us to follow in Jesus' footsteps. In his *Sermon on the Mount,* Wesley described the many ways in which acts of devotion as well as acts of mercy are enabled by what is removed from the heart by the Lord—our sinful tendencies. Wesley indicates that just as hunger and thirst are the strongest bodily appetites, the hunger and thirst of the soul for true righteousness drive a human being to find that which he or she ultimately desires. Nothing but God himself can satisfy a soul that thirsts for true religion. Good works and outward expressions of care are only manifestations of his inward state.[1] When a soul finds satisfaction and fulfillment in God, it will overflow from within like a fountain and the person will become concerned for those who are still without God in the world.[2]

Based on James 1, Wesley insisted that true religion is most visible in how the poor are treated—an indication that our hearts are in the right place. One of his deepest concerns was to help Christians recognize the importance of charity to and solidarity with the poor as evidence of a rich spirituality. For example, in another one of his sermons, *The Scripture Way of Salvation*, Wesley affirms that "works of mercy, whether they relate to the bodies or souls of men, such as feeding the hungry, clothing the naked, entertaining the stranger . . . are necessary to full sanctification."[3]

The church's authenticity will be most clearly perceived in our treatment of the least of these—the widows, the foreigners, and the poor. The role of witnessing can be described in a multiplicity of ways, but sharing the good news with the poor means that good news should replace bad news. That is, if people are hungry, they can be fed. If they are illiterate, they can have access to education. If they are ill, they should have the right to medical care. This is what the kingdom of God is about—a place where the broken are made whole, the oppressed can find freedom, and the hungry are satisfied with good things.

1. Wesley, *Sermon on the Mount* 2, Part II, par. 3.
2. Wesley, *Sermon on the Mount* 2, Part III, par. 1.
3. Wesley, *The Scripture Way of Salvation*, Part III, par. 10.

A Guiding Light unto Our Path

Jesus inherited from his Hebrew forefathers a strong sense of solidarity and a firm commitment to mercy, justice, and love for those lacking in material goods. Throughout the four Gospels, we find a Jesus who is concerned with the poor and the marginalized. Liberation theologians believe that Jesus had a "preference for the poor."[4] Indeed, many theologians have reflected on the relevance that the gospel brings to all dimensions of human life. Walter Rauschenbusch formulated a theology that highlighted careful attention to socio-economic needs, affirming that "the social gospel needs a theology to make it effective, but theology needs the social gospel to vitalize it."[5] Martin Luther King Jr. directed his efforts to the fulfillment of this task. He once said, "We can talk all we want about saving souls from hell and preaching the pure and simple gospel, but unless we preach the social gospel our evangelistic gospel will be meaningless."[6] By bringing a message of liberation to the oppressed and a message of hope from the chains of racism and economic struggles, Martin Luther King Jr. was able to challenge the social practices of his time and speak prophetically to the hearts of people. King believed that the greatest struggle hindering the *shalom* that God desired people to enjoy was between the forces of justice trying to end corrupt systems and the forces of injustice trying to maintain them.[7]

Both spiritual and structural forces threaten to destroy the social harmony characteristic of *shalom.* John Stott says, "*Shalom* is exemplified in such areas as the battle against racism, the humanization of industrial relations, the overcoming of class divisions, community development, and the quest for an ethic of honesty and integrity in business and other professions."[8] These efforts should be grounded on the promise of God's blessing and

---

4. Ferm, *Third World Liberation Theologies,* 11.

5. Rauschenbusch, *Theology for the Social Gospel,* 1.

6. King, *The Measure of a Man,* 3.

7. King, *The Measure of a Man,* 7.

8. Stott, *Christian Mission,* 18.

on God's desire that all peoples may enjoy fellowship with him and live in reconciliation with each other (Eph 2:13–22).

The writer of Ecclesiastes describes the state of the world in which he lived as one where "wickedness exists in the place of justice" (Eccl 3:16). This condition has not ceased. In fact, it has increased. The teacher in Ecclesiastes adds, "Whoever loves money never has enough; whoever loves wealth is never satisfied with their income" (Eccl 5:10). The love of money is contrasted with the gift of wealth given by God for a greater purpose: "When God gives someone wealth and possessions, and the ability to enjoy them, to accept their lot and be happy in their toil—this is a gift of God" (Eccl 6:18). Proverbs also sheds light on this ethical issue (Prov 13:11, 17:16), arguing that money dwindles away if it is not properly used.

For that reason, monetary resources must be channeled into purposeful causes instead of being utilized for personal gain. The early church, along with the formative practices that led to spiritual growth, exhibited a genuine concern for the poor. Even when great monetary resources were not at their disposal, the disciples gave what they had available, such as the authority to lift the sick out of their places of bodily poverty (Acts 3:6). These concerns became the wheels that kept the church moving forward and the fuel that kept it alive. Certainly, God desires to meet our needs and give us the desires of our heart, but our desires are often set on wrong things—things that God cannot promise to fulfill.

One secular tool that reinforces the idea that people desire to fulfill a higher purpose in life is psychologist Abraham Maslow's hierarchy of human needs. Maslow contended that human life progresses from meeting a lower level of basic needs until it satisfies its highest level of need, which he called self-actualization. Although Maslow did not specifically design this hierarchy to be applied to spiritual needs, his concept shows that individuals intrinsically desire to advance in life and find satisfaction in ways that go beyond common and mundane needs. This satisfaction seems unreachable to many, especially those who lack the resources to meet lower needs, such as belonging and safety. But our highest need can be met and fulfilled through a dynamic relationship with God and by abiding in his love. A biblical and theological notion of self-actualization may be best reframed as self-*giving* love, for loving God and others is the most certain way to find satisfaction and fulfillment in life.

The Dimensions of Poverty

When God created the world, he created it in perfect order. Sin disrupted God's creation, and the effects of the fall caused a rupture in our fellowship and intimacy with God. But this was not the only consequence. Sin affected every area of our human existence, from the economic, relational, and ecological to the religious, political, and social aspects of life. In the words of Steve Corbett and Brian Fikkert, "Every human being is suffering from a poverty of spiritual intimacy, a poverty of being, a poverty of community, and a poverty of stewardship."[9] Behind our selfish and sinful tendencies are evil forces, rampant in the world, wreaking havoc in the lives of individuals and their families. This reality has led to a vicious cycle that has affected the core of our being and may seem, at times, impossible to break. Broken systems exist at the micro level (i.e., family systems) as well as the macro level (i.e., economic systems), deeply impacting our lives.

While the concept of poverty has often been taken to imply economic deprivation, it can be understood in different ways and extended to many other areas of life. G. Ellis identifies several types of poverty that help classify the dimensions of experiential poverty. First, there is *economic poverty*, which refers to the lack of resources available to increase a group's well-being. These are not exclusively related to financial concerns but extend to the technological areas of life as well, as many individuals around the world lack access to innovative resources that facilitate daily operations. The second type is *social poverty*, which describes the lack of social networks or supporting structures that enable opportunities for

9. Corbett and Fikkert, *When Helping Hurts*, 59.

advancement through social capital and which is often external-ized because of generational patterns. The third is *political poverty,* which relates to the lack of access to a fair share of resources that might be available to the society as a whole, including representation in positions of power that offer possibilities of making decisions for minority groups from their own lived experiences and perspectives. The final category is *psychological poverty,* which has an effect on individuals whose brain chemistry has been affected as a result of other's painful actions or arisen as a result of biological conditions outside of their control and who have no access to proper medical care.[10]

The most pronounced category of poverty, however, is the economic one, which encompasses income poverty and material deprivation.[11] These stressors have far-reaching consequences for children, teenagers, families, and entire groups of people and can be debilitating, leading to other types of poverty. Because poverty is multi-dimensional, poverty reduction requires different kinds of developmental interventions to bring people out of its trenches.

Most anti-poverty interventions tend to focus on similar outcomes, but the criteria often differ in implementation, making programs difficult to sustain long-term. Several questions call for further reflection. Should the focus be on activities that reduce poverty today or those that might help alleviate it in the future? Would it be more efficient to seek to minimize the effects of poverty on a thousand individuals for a single year or permanently lift one hundred people out of poverty long-term? These questions are not easy to answer, and the answers will differ according to particular contexts and circumstances as well as the type of resources available to meet such needs. Because sustainability is often sacrificed on the altar of quick fixes, we must consider the perception of the assistance provided to a particular group as to how it is received by the community. Does it build capacity or do the benefits last only while the funding or resources are provided? Are the effects sustained after the assistance and intervention end?

10. Ellis, "Dimensions of Poverty," 242–50.

11. Schenck–Fontaine and Panico, *Many Kinds,* 2279.

Is the aid eroding local capacity or leading to its expansion? These questions should be evaluated case by case so as to ensure the most meaningful and enduring impact.

Managing symptoms often supersedes addressing the root causes of poverty, because it takes more time, energy, personnel, and resources to address situations from the ground up. But the local church has the opportunity to address and transform root behaviors through personal relationships with those who are on the receiving end of benevolent efforts. We cannot expect the church to fix all the ills in the world, and Jesus himself said that poverty would continue to be a reality in our earthly journey (Matt 26:11). Nevertheless, through missional endeavors, compassionate ministries focused on crisis intervention, and temporary relief, the church can serve as the hands and feet of Jesus in significant ways.

Development and rehabilitation are not always the answer to every problem either. There is certainly a place for the extension and provision of relief initiatives when situations that arise from sudden and drastic calamities call for such efforts. And that is where the church may be most effective. Through education, training, and support, entire communities can rise up, even if temporarily, out of the situations that have long plagued them. One of the best ways in which the church can make a long-lasting impact is through the formation of cross-cultural partnerships that seek to share resources, ideas, and perspectives embedded in local networks. The capacity for sharing resources, information, and support has never been more available and enriching than in today's world, where mutuality in mission efforts has continued to be on the rise.

Cross-Cultural Partnerships

Part of God's design for restoring the cosmos is to bring his people into relationships that are mutually beneficial. This is not an easy task. On one hand, most Westerners live in a culture that values independence; on the other hand, the Majority World has historically been affected by systems that have kept them in cycles of dependence. By relying on God's grace, however, we can move to a place of interdependence with others where the goods exchanged might vary in monetary value but should be considered of equal importance.

Today's globalized world requires an interconnected church to carry out God's mission. For that reason, cross-cultural partnerships can be a means by which the church demonstrates the relational nature of God. The changing role that American churches have adopted in mission endeavors in recent years, shifting from senders to supporters, must be understood in the context of global connectedness. Wuthnow remarks, "A body is organically connected, [and] it functions best when the particular contributions of its parts work together."[12] As a result, global Christianity will thrive when cooperation ensues to meet the needs of the world. Working together may still be a challenge, as conflict can often arise from cultural differences over social values, expectations, leadership styles, and decision-making processes. Nevertheless, with cultural competence and the help of cultural brokers, cross-cultural partnerships can become an effective tool in missions.

Among the benefits of cross-cultural partnerships are the relational ties that lead to the growth and development of both parties. Although resource sharing often includes providing monetary resources to meet specific material needs, the partnerships can also focus on other meaningful projects, such as joint initiatives of service and social justice, or equipping and training. Even when the benefits of entering into a partnership might outweigh its challenges, several potential threats will need to be addressed, as discussed below.

Paternalism, Power, and Money

One of the issues that often emerges in relationships where socioeconomic imbalances are present is paternalism, which can be defined as "acting for the good of another person without the person's

12. Wuthnow, *Boundless Faith*, 61.

consent."[13] Paternalism often occurs when leaders in positions of power and greater financial resources assume that they possess superior knowledge, skills, and experience relative to local leaders or people who have less power and financial resources. This perspective often leads to the exertion of strong control over the less advantaged in decision making. In missions, paternalism is often connected to colonialism, the historical period during which Global North governments occupied and conquered various parts of the world. Although we live in a post-colonial age, a colonial mentality tends to linger, and it is usually the last thing to go. An inherent sense of superiority can often lead individuals in positions of power to make decisions with ulterior motives.

The issue of paternalism and how to overcome it has been debated by generations of mission scholars. Rufus Anderson (1796–1880) and Henry Venn (1796–1873), for instance, developed indigenous church principles known as the "Three-Self" formula,[14] which operated under the premise that money, power, and the expansion of the church should be devoid of dependence on outside sources. Although these principles are suitable for church planting in pioneer areas, little was said about how established churches should relate to each other once they reached maturity or economic stability.

Despite the promising results and ventures that can come about through various forms of collaboration, some leaders and researchers have voiced concerns where perceptions of paternalistic attitudes and colonial patterns may still predominate in global efforts.[15] Ellen Moodie, drawing on her research on sister communities in El Salvador and the United States, argues that socio-economic gaps between cultures are a necessary evil and function as a pre-condition for partnerships to work effectively. She believes that "the disparities between the visitors and the

13. Lederleitner, *Cross-Cultural*, 78.

14. The principles of the Three-Selfs are embedded in the idea that indigenous churches ought to become self-supporting, self-governing, and self-propagating.

15. Borthwick, *Western Christians*, 150.

visited—economic, geographic, cultural, political—are not something to overcome."[16] Rather, they are something to acknowledge as a gap needing a bridge. Janel Bakker holds a contrasting perspective, viewing challenges such as structural imbalances of power, the difficulty of effective cross-cultural communication, and the instability of interpersonal relationships as factors that can prevent effective reciprocal efforts.[17] Conflicts over differences threaten to tear teams apart and compromise their efforts, while economic and social barriers handicap relationships. Although the socio-economic gap between Global North and Global South congregations may be a necessary precondition for the *establishment* of a global relationship, it must continually be recognized and duly addressed for the *sustainability* of the relationship.

Furthermore, dependency has also become a point of contention to consider. On one side are those who favor the "self-supporting" formula in order to allow greater initiative, believing that charity may destroy dignity and that dependency may contribute to fatalistic beliefs that make it difficult to break from the mentality of "once poor always poor." On the other side are those who propose an "interdependent" approach to partnerships, believing that God calls those with vast resources to share wisely and generously with those who have less.

From Dependency into Interdependence

In mission circles, the risk of fostering dependency is a major concern. Two main camps hold differing positions in the dependency debate. One camp believes that indigenous ministries should be "self-reliant" or "independent" from foreign funding in order to avoid the syndrome or fallacy of inadequate collective agency or self-initiative. Among the voices who embrace this conservative view are Glenn Schwartz and Robertson McQuilkin. Schwartz believes that the solution to dependency should not be determined

16. Moodie, "Inequality," 147.

17. Bakker, *Sister Churches*, 184.

arbitrarily. He affirms, "When they take that bold move, the results can be as dramatic."[18] In a more recent publication, *When Charity Destroys Dignity*, Schwartz expands on his views, asserting that the solution to unhealthy dependency is becoming self-reliant. He defines this term as being able to "use and multiply the resources that God has put closely at hand" while ensuring sustainability at the same time.[19] Similarly, McQuilkin finds no biblical justification for supporting the ministry of other churches, and he calls for steering away from pouring funds into foreign churches' projects unless money is sent to assist the poor specifically.[20]

Although these writers' intentions are good and helpful, they dismiss the importance of sharing resources that might potentially be used to expand the kingdom of God in ways that otherwise would not be possible. They also ignore the reality that a great number of churches in the Majority World are in the beginning stages of development and do not possess the financial capacity to pour resources into their projects. While the goal should be to foster self-support, it does not seem logical to expect that this would happen immediately, but it should be the goal.

On the other side of the spectrum are those who advocate "mutual dependence" or "interdependence," such as John Rowell and Daniel Rickett. Rowell calls for "a renewed sense of global stewardship and a radical redirection of resources to meet the chronic needs of the global poor."[21] He builds his argument around the need to restore generosity and redefine sustainability, contending, "Whenever funds are given without regard to the capacity of nationals to manage, maintain, or multiply the investments made, or to make their own contributions along the way, dependency is a distinct possibility."[22] Rowell refutes the misconception that has been created around the Three-Self formula, asserting that refraining from giving to under-resourced brothers and sisters around

18. Schwartz, "Cutting the Apron," 240.

19. Schwartz, *Charity Destroys*, 38.

20. McQuilkin, "Stop Sending Money," 59.

21. Rowell, *To Give*, 14.

22. Rowell, *To Give*, 16.

the world is "self-serving" and not coherent with the biblical principle of radical generosity.

A common misconception is that the giving of financial assistance to a partner may lead to unhealthy dependence on such gifts. However, Westerners themselves often depend on funds for their mission work, whether it comes via their salary or the generous giving of donors. Thus, a double standard arises, where limits are placed on Majority World Christians but not on Global North Christians. Rickett affirms that "interdependency starts by doing away with double standards" in order to deal "with the real causes of unhealthy dependency."[23] Unhealthy dependency consists of relying on outside sources at the expense of local autonomy, responsibility, and resourcefulness. This should serve as a reminder that other ways can have long-lasting effects that are more positive and constructive in nature. As a way to bridge both camps in this discussion, Craig Ott concludes that "financial assistance, even when motivated by compassion, should not undermine individual willingness to work and provide for one's own needs."[24] Compassion should be coupled with proper education. One of the most compassionate things we can do for those in financial need is to instruct, help steward, and work toward indigenous initiative by putting in place sustainable mechanisms so people might enjoy the fruit of their labor and take pride in their own efforts.

Global and Local Mission

As churches in North America become increasingly aware of the dire needs around the world, engaging in local nor global missions has never been easier. Equipping the congregation for action is necessary and foundational to allow God's people to exercise the gifts they have been given and get involved in opportunities to serve the poor, whether abroad or at home. Actually, the 21st-century church must be *glocal* in its mission. Cultivating relationships

23. Rickett, "Walk with Me," 164.

24. Ott, "Missions and Money," 8.

at home and abroad, experiencing evangelistic fervor firsthand, and engaging in missional acts through compassionate ministries can function as motivating factors guiding believers to embrace a life of missional action without being restricted to a geographical location. For example, short-term mission trips might provide an opportunity to witness firsthand the conditions of the poor and the realities of the Majority World, which might make us more frugal and mindful of how we employ the resources God has given us. But we don't have to travel across the globe to find situations that need our attention and service. Churches can partner with community-based organizations in their own communities to encourage their services. Many nonprofit organizations and community groups address poverty reduction and alleviation, including ministries targeting low-income populations, pregnancy resource centers, after-school care programs, tutoring, mentoring for children at risk, and more.

Missional living requires us to be equipped for ministry. For fellowship to be enriching, sustaining, and prevailing, one must remain open to the gifts that the Spirit bestows upon us according to his will. The Holy Spirit provides and grants gifts to everyone (1 Cor 7:7; 12:29–30), but he allocates them according to his will (1 Cor 12:11; Rom 12:4–6). The desire to help those in need or show mercy is a gift associated with compassion. If someone has the gift of giving, he or she must do so generously (Rom 12:8). This gift is a reflection of the generosity of God who gives the Spirit without limit (John 3:34). Likewise, the gift of mercy is given by God so that we might use it to bless others. Because the Lord is full of compassion and mercy (Jas 5:11), he bestows this gift generously among his people. Mercy and compassion walk hand in hand, and we don't have to wait to receive these gifts to engage in missional activities, for these gifts are a part of the fruit of the Spirit where love, joy, and goodness allow us to work out our faith through deeds. With the challenges of urbanization, a rapidly changing social landscape, and the increase of brokenness in many ways and at many levels, opportunities to serve the poor have never been more readily available and needed.

9

Tuning in to Spiritual Dynamics

WITH THE IMPACT OF globalization, the rise of Eastern spirituality in the West, the emergence of the New Age Movement, and the influence of Pentecostalism around the world, Christians have become increasingly aware of dynamics in the spiritual realm, which have presented another dimension of mission focus. The last several decades have seen an explosion of books and articles published from a variety of perspectives on spiritual warfare in particular, along with the emergence of ministries and strategies combating unseen forces through prayer. Flourishing ministries have appeared almost universally, seeking to bring healing to those claiming to be spiritually oppressed and confused. Regrettably, some eager individuals who have been quick to offer relief to hurting individuals have delved into the practice of freedom ministry[1] without due preparation and education, failing to undertake adequate theological reflection to clarify their strategies. Individuals under demonic oppression are often misunderstood by the church and treated as if they were insane or in need of psychiatric intervention. In recent years, however, the continual awareness of the spirit world has led more of the Christian community to recognize

1. Freedom ministry is a prayer-based approach that utilizes the spiritual gift of discernment and the authority of Christ to bring deep healing to Christians who have experienced spiritual setbacks and emotional wounding.

that many problems in life stem from a supernatural cause that affects the natural world. Most of the Christian community in the West, however, remains suspicious and ignorant and does not have the necessary understanding of spiritual dynamics to help those who are caught in cycles of torment by demonic assault.

With the continual rise of these types of ministries in local churches and parachurch organizations, we must pay careful attention to determine the most appropriate way to assist affected individuals. Although Christians inevitably experience the attacks of the enemy, not everyone suffers under his continual oppression. Individuals who were once involved in gangs, the occult, or have been victims of witchcraft need spiritual intervention so that they may move freely from a past of darkness into the hope of a renewed life.

I recognize that a myriad of diverse positions have been proposed over time; therefore, it would be presumptuous to think I could settle the issues here. Nevertheless, the aim is to bring to light the main voices behind the topics of spiritual warfare, the practice of deliverance, and inner healing in order to offer theological reflections by which to respond to the challenges and opportunities these ministries present. Many experts on mission have sought to raise awareness of these issues among Western Christians who often dismiss them as matters of mere speculation or conjecture.[2] To extend the grace and healing of Christ to individuals who have had spiritual experiences connected to the occult or who come from places predisposed to power encounters, these issues must be taken seriously and addressed with adequate training.

Spiritual Warfare

Writers on spiritual warfare are numerous. A quick examination of publications reveals the vastness of published materials on the topic. Some of the most widely read works among the lay populace are Christian fiction. For instance, Frank Peretti drew an international

2. See for example Ott et al., *Encountering Theology of Mission* (2010); Pocock, *The Changing Face of World Missions* (2005).

audience to his writings in the late 1980s through novels such as *This Present Darkness* and *Piercing the Darkness*. More recently, *New York Times* bestselling author Priscilla Shirer released an epic series titled *The Prince Warriors*, bringing to life the invisible war in the spiritual realm.

Most nonfiction writers on spiritual warfare have focused on providing a readable treatment of the spiritual battle that rages against our souls, intertwining biblical evidence with real-life experiences to offer practical steps to help individuals be victorious in their Christian life. In addition to popular writings, a growing number of scholars have engaged in academic study of this topic, organizing conferences and worldwide consultations, and thereby lending credence to this area.[3] What follows here is a brief categorization of the literature on spiritual warfare so as to systematically organize the various views on the topic.

Truth-Encounter Approach

The first category of publications on spiritual warfare consists of those advocating a truth-encounter approach, teaching individuals how to apply biblical truth as they combat the attacks of the enemy. Perhaps the most influential author in this camp is Neil T. Anderson, whose *Steps to Freedom in Christ*, *The Bondage Breaker*, and *Victory over the Darkness* help Christians recognize their authority and identity in Christ. Anderson writes, "Satan is a defeated foe; therefore, his power is limited, but he still has the ability to deceive the whole world. Because Satan's primary weapon is the lie, your defense against him is the truth. Dealing with Satan is not a power encounter; it is a truth encounter."[4] Other reliable writings representing this camp are Scott Moreau's *Essentials of Spiritual Warfare*

---

3. One example is the Lausanne consultation on spiritual conflict, entitled "Deliver Us from Evil," which convened in August 2000 and included academic theologians, missiologists and practitioners engaged in ministry. More information about the work of this consultation and the various papers presented can be read in *Deliver Us from Evil: An Uneasy Frontier in Christian Mission.*

4. Anderson, *Victory Over the Darkness,* 166.

and Timothy Warner's *Spiritual Warfare*. This approach has not aroused controversy, as it centers on helping individuals find freedom by renewing their minds with the truth of Christ (John 8:32).

Power-Encounter Approach

The second group of writers has approached spiritual warfare in terms of a power encounter, predicating their views upon the reality that our struggle is not against flesh and blood but against the powers of this dark world (Eph 6:12). Charles Kraft, a Christian anthropologist, has written extensively on spiritual warfare from this perspective. In *Defeating Dark Angels,* Kraft asserts that we must "work in the power of God to bring freedom to the afflicted person with a maximum of love and a minimum of craziness."[5] Proponents of this approach believe that supernatural activity has not passed away with the age of the apostles as many cessationists[6] hold, but that through the use of spiritual gifts, such as discernment between spirits (1 Cor 12:10), those living in spiritual bondage can be set free.

Marguerite Kraft writes, "Western worldviews also limit people's ability to recognize the possibility of humans using evil power to harm other people."[7] Certainly, it is not always the case that demonic attacks are at the root of the problems we experience in life, but it could sometimes be the case. That is why spiritual discernment becomes a key part in recognizing and addressing what may be at work in a given situation.

More recently, the number of writers adopting this approach has been growing. Kynan Bridges is among them. His *Overcoming Familiar Spirits* and *Unlocking the Code of the Supernatural* provide helpful biblical insights as to how to defeat unseen forces that perpetually interfere in the lives of believers, especially when we have strongholds that give the enemy the right to wage war against

5. Kraft, *Defeating Dark Angels*, 11.

6. Cessationists maintain that the divine provision of miracles and displays of supernatural power ended with the era of the apostles in the New Testament.

7. Kraft, *Understanding Spiritual Power,* 36.

our soul. Sin must be confessed, bitterness released, and forgiveness offered through a process, in order to keep our hearts free and move to a healthy place.

Scholars

As discussions of spiritual warfare began to rise in prominence in various inter-denominational circles, researchers and academics were drawn to studying spiritual dynamics in the contemporary world and from a biblical perspective. Perhaps the most influential in academic circles is Walter Wink, whose trilogy *Naming the Powers* presents a biblical discussion while emphasizing the socio-structural side of evil and spiritual warfare. Ed Murphy's *Handbook for Spiritual Warfare* offers one of the most comprehensive expositions on the topic. His combination of biblical knowledge, field experience, and theological reflection has made this contribution a highly valued resource. Gregory Boyd is another theologian working from a warfare perspective. His compelling work *God at War* wrestles primarily with the problem of suffering and evil, treating it thoroughly from a biblical-theological perspective grounded in the Old Testament.

Clinton Arnold approaches the topic primarily from a biblical-historical perspective. In *Powers of Darkness: Principalities and Powers in Paul's Letters,* Arnold contends that the New Testament views spiritual forces not as impersonal structures, but as personal beings that seek to deceive individuals. In *3 Crucial Questions about Spiritual Warfare*, Arnold offers an extensive articulation of these important concerns and reflects, "To think that a Christian could avoid spiritual warfare is like imagining that a gardener could avoid dealing with weeds."[8] Therefore, he argues that Christians must be adequately equipped to contend with the forces of evil present in the world.

In recent years, missiologists have become leading voices in the arena, linking biblical reflection and practical means to

8. Arnold, *Crucial Questions*, 19.

illumine methodological approaches. An oft-referenced article by Christian anthropologist Paul Hiebert, titled *The Flaw of the Excluded Middle*, contends that Westerners have been constrained in their perception of the existential reality of spirits, angels, demons, and ancestors because of a blind spot in their view of reality. Hiebert's call for a holistic theology that includes "a theology of spirits and invisible powers of this world" was coupled with a warning that such a theology could unintentionally lead to a "Christianized form of animism in which spirits and magic are used to explain everything."[9] His thoughtful appeal for a balanced approach was well received in evangelical circles, giving impetus for a broader missiological understanding that takes spiritual dynamics seriously. Missiologists Craig Ott and Stephen Strauss side with this understanding by affirming it succinctly: "Mission theology is incomplete without a theology of the excluded middle that is rooted in Scripture."[10] This theology must recognize the presence of spiritual forces and the manifestation of spiritual dynamics while emphasizing God's ultimate supremacy over creation, including the spirit world.

Many scholars have contributed reflections in defense of the experiences of modern-day individuals whose claims of spirit possession seem analogous to biblical accounts. New Testament scholars have pointed out that many of the accounts in the modern world display a striking resemblance to the reports of New Testament eyewitnesses. Among these scholars are Craig Keener, Richard Bauckham, and Joy Vaughan. Their conclusions help us make sense of the pervasiveness of behaviors seemingly attributable to spirit possession from around the world.[11]

9. Hiebert, "Flaw of the Excluded Middle," 42.

10. Ott et al., *Encountering Theology of Mission*, 254.

11. See for instance Keener, "Spirit Possession" (2010); Bauckham, *Jesus and Eyewitness* (2006); and Vaughan, *Phenomenal Phenomena* (2023).

Spiritual Healers

Two interrelated streams can be unearthed among practitioners in the field working from a warfare perspective—namely, "inner healing" and "deliverance." Agnes Sanford is the forerunner of the inner healing movement and a trailblazer in the art of healing prayer. Many of her early works, however, such as *The Healing Light*, were heavily influenced by the New Thought[12] movement, leaving her open to criticism of unbiblical undertones in her writings. Her beliefs about the healing power of God were replaced by more biblically sound ideas in later writings, such as in *The Healing Gifts of the Spirit*.

Sanford's pioneering work paved the way for the maturation and concretization of her ideas over time. Theologians and practitioners such as David Seamands and Terry Wardle, theologians and avid writers on the topic, shed light on the value of a Christo-centric pastoral approach to healing. In *Healing for Damaged Emotions* and *Wounds That Heal*, Seamands provides a careful explanation of how God desires to bring healing to damaged emotions and painful memories, comforting individuals in areas where they have suffered as a result of trauma. Likewise, Wardle's extensive work on healing prayer provides an important foundation to help broken people find wholeness in Christ. His approach is based on years of careful research as well as his own personal experience with formational prayer (his term for the process of inner healing). Wardle's general style aligns with a pastoral counseling and spiritual formation approach, highlighting in particular the role of prayer and the work of the Holy Spirit to bring healing to a person's emotional and mental capacities. His books *Healing Care, Healing Prayer*, and *Wounded: How to Find Wholeness and Inner Healing Through Him* are among the best selections on this important topic.

12. The New Thought movement was based on the teachings of Phineas Quimby, who maintained that illness originated in the mind as a consequence of erroneous beliefs and that a mind open to God's wisdom and to positive thinking could overcome any illness.

The second stream of thought in the category of literature about spiritual healing consists of people who specialize in deliverance models of healing. Deliverance models seek to help individuals find freedom from demonic oppression. Among some of the most thorough and helpful perspectives are *Deliverance from Evil Spirits* by Francis MacNutt, who was a leading voice in the Catholic charismatic renewal; *Deliverance and Inner Healing* by John Loren Sandford and Mark Sandford, leaders of Elijah Rain Ministries; *Healing Through Deliverance* by Peter Horrobin; *With Gentle Authority: A Manual for Inner Healing and Freedom Ministry* by Tim Howard and Brian Burke, working in the Wesleyan tradition; and *The X-Manual: Exousia—a Comprehensive Handbook on Deliverance and Exorcism* by Peter Bellini, a seminary professor who bridges academic understanding with practical tools for engaging in deliverance ministries.

Questionable Writings

Not all voices on spiritual warfare have solid scriptural foundations. Some concerning books have appeared as well, contributing to the already high level of controversy over this type of ministry. An example is Rebecca Brown, who has written considerably on how to overcome the power of the enemy. Her book *He Came to Set the Captives Free* describes the story of Elaine, a satanist and leading witch in the United States who converted to Christianity. The publication of Elaine's story resulted in threats to Brown's life because of Elaine's previous satanist connections. This book, although it seeks to help people recognize and combat the reality of satanic attacks, is not theologically sound. Many statements in her books reveal faulty theology upon which she predicates her concepts of spiritual warfare. For example, she believes that God the "Father never experienced weakness, so he usually gets angry when his people are weak."[13] This is clearly a misrepresentation of the love of the Father, who reminds us that his grace is enough and

13. Brown, *He Came to Set the Captives Free*, 17.

that his "power is perfected in weakness" (2 Cor 12:9). Some of Brown's statements lead to fear and are not grounded in Scripture, such as her declarations that curses come from God. As an example she cites the lack of fertility in women or men and economic collapse as God's "direct injury" to those who disobey him while claiming that "God gives Satan the legal right to send demons onto people to destroy them."[14]

Approaches to spiritual warfare and healing must be taken seriously but treated with caution. A balanced and scriptural view is necessary as we approach this topic. Undue emphasis on unseen forces can lead, as has happened in the past, to the emergence of extreme strategies such as "Strategic-Level Spiritual Warfare" with its focus on "territorial spirits."[15] While these topics have been long addressed by practitioners in the field, they have also attracted a fair share of scholarly critique.[16]

Scriptural Basis for the Practice of Freedom Ministries

The victory of Christ on the cross was enough to defeat death, the last enemy, making it possible for Christians to have victory over the enemy through the redemptive work of Christ. However, as long as we live on this side of eternity, the enemy will seek to tempt and deceive us, for his mission to "steal, kill, and destroy" is very

14. Brown and Yoder, *Unbroken Curses*, 18.

15. Many missiologists, including Peter Wagner, Charles Kraft, and George Otis Jr., have reasoned that if evil spirits could interfere in the lives of individuals, entire people groups could be held captive by "territorial spirits." Thus, for the light of the gospel to penetrate the hearts of individuals and enable receptivity to the gospel, these evil powers need to be exorcised. Although the reality of demonic spirits associated with territories has a scriptural basis (see Daniel 10:12–13, 20), there is not scriptural evidence showing that Christians are called to engage these territorial spirits through prayer or that they have the authority to cast them out.

16. See Twibell, "Strategic-Level Spiritual Warfare: A Theological Assessment of its Premises and Practices" for a detailed evaluation of this strategy and debate.

real and rampant (John 10:10). For that reason, we must recognize not only our authority in Christ but also the power of God to defeat the enemy's schemes at every turn, pulling down strongholds and casting out everything that sets itself up against the knowledge of God (2 Cor 10:5).

The Scriptures describe the grand narrative of salvation history that God initiated after sin entered the world. God desires to rescue us from the enslavement of sin and remake us in his image and likeness so that we may experience his never-ending love and become conduits of his grace in a broken world. The Scriptures depict Satan as the enemy of our souls, opposing everything that is meaningful to the heart of God, prowling like a lion and seeking someone to devour. An invisible cosmic battle rages between the kingdom of God and the kingdom of Satan, along with an inward battle between what the Spirit desires to cultivate in us and what the flesh desires. In this struggle, we can decide to yield to God, confess our sin, and turn away from evil, or we can continue to love sinful habits or hide our pain.

Jesus' own ministry was marked by encounters with evil forces, unclean spirits, and temptation. He was tempted not only at the beginning of his public ministry as the Spirit led him into the wilderness (Luke 4:1–13), but also as he neared the end of his earthly ministry (Matt 26:36–45). He encountered evil forces and unclean spirits in individuals such as Mary Magdalene (Mark 16:19), the Gadarene demoniac (Mark 5:2–20), the man who was mute (Matt 9:32–34), the boy who had experienced seizures since early childhood (Matt 17:14–22), the woman bound by a spirit of infirmity (Luke 13:10–17), and many others. Jesus freed individuals who had been tormented by the devil and plagued by circumstances and situations outside their control.

When Jesus rose from the dead and appeared to his disciples, he commissioned them to "go sinto all the world and preach the gospel to all creation," promising that "signs [would] accompany those who believe: In my name they will drive out demons . . . they will place their hands on sick people, and they will recover" (Mark 16:15–18). This commission was not only for the disciples. When

Jesus appeared to Saul along the road to Damascus, he gave him the same authority, and the book of Acts gives ample evidence of how mightily Paul was used by God, "so that even handkerchiefs and aprons that had touched him were taken to the sick, and their illnesses were cured and the evil spirits left them" (Acts 18:12). The same commission applies to all Christians today who through a Spirit-filled life and gentle approach, and in the mighty name of Jesus, are given the power and the authority to unmask the evil spirits that interfere in peoples' lives.

"Demonization" in Believers

The possibility that Christians may be subject to the influence of the enemy (i.e., demonized) is perhaps the single most controversial aspect of spiritual warfare. This aspect deserves full attention, but further biblical and empirical research is necessary to evaluate this understanding. To begin, a biblically-based expert in the field asserts that "Scripture, church history, and contemporary experience show that under unusual conditions of sin, either their own or the sin of others against them, some believers become demonized."[17] Most Christians, however, reject the possibility of demonization in true believers, arguing that no life indwelt by the Holy Spirit can be under the influence of the enemy to that extent.

Clinton Arnold uses the spatial metaphor of a house to show that while Christ may be present in a room of the house, intruders can be present in other rooms of the house. He reflects, "As long as the pornographic literature remains hidden on the bathroom shelf, the spirit feels that it has every right to remain. All the while the illicit relationship continues in the bedroom, another evil denizen is determined to stay."[18] Charles Kraft uses the illustration of "rats" to describe how demons are attracted to the "garbage" hidden in some rooms of the house into which Christ has not yet been

17. Murphy, *Handbook*, 429.

18. Arnold, *Crucial Questions*, 87.

invited.[19] As we yield to Christ's influence and let him occupy those spaces, the garbage and rats are cleaned out. Arnold concludes that while a "Christian cannot be owned and controlled by a demon," individuals, both Christian and non-Christian, can be "influenced by evil spirits."[20] Christians cannot be demon-possessed, for they are owned by the Spirit of God. But when certain sources remain unhealed or a foothold is given to the enemy (Eph 4:26) and not confessed, strongholds develop (2 Cor 10:3–5) that leave Christians susceptible to the enemy's influence in their lives to varying degrees.

Some experts on this topic argue that any level of activity that a demonic being exerts against a Christian can be treated as "demonization." Some hold the view that demonization takes different forms, ranging from harassment, oppression, and affliction to bondage. Regardless of the terminology used, there are evil forces that wage war against our soul and must be overcome through prayer and the word of God. Such language should not be used carelessly, so as to avoid provoking conversations that may contribute to an overwhelming sense of fear or dehumanization in victims who are already experiencing inner turmoil.

The Promise of Abundant Life

Life brings painful and hurtful experiences, which create fractures in our soul that may lead to the formation of dysfunctional behaviors intended to mitigate, cover up, minimize, or escape the pain we feel inside if our pain continues to go unaddressed. These may be strongholds of addiction, perfectionism, criticism, consumerism, pessimism, ambition or approval. These boulders are safeguarded by certain layers of emotion, such as fear, anger, grief, and pride.

Jesus insisted that to follow him, we must "deny our self" (Matt 16:24). Denying our self simply means that we reject that within us which has been marred by sinful tendencies, generational

---

19. See Kraft, *Two Hours of Freedom* (2010) for a thorough and detailed description of this approach.

20. Arnold, *Crucial Questions*, 88.

patterns, and personal choices not in alignment with God's character or his desires for us. The promise stands true: he who began a good work will complete it (Phil 1:6), for Jesus has come so that we may have life and enjoy it abundantly (John 10:10) and he has come to set us free from sin and the grip of the enemy (1 John 3:8).

The journey toward healing is a process enabled by the Holy Spirit, with the support and care of other Christians. In some cases where strongholds may have developed over time due to severe trauma, sinful tendencies, the behavior of others, or involvement in occult practices, deliverance prayers may be necessary as well as professional counseling. Individuals dealing with emotional instability or mental health issues may require more than prayer for inner healing to continue growing in their spiritual journey. Prayer will only open the door to release and confess what needs to be addressed. Henri Nouwen expresses the inner healing that our soul desires in this way: "You have to move gradually from crying outward—crying out for people who you think can fulfill your needs—to crying inward, to the place where you can let yourself be held and carried by God, who has become incarnate in the humanity of those who love you in community."[21]

It would be misleading and simplistic to assume that all of our issues could be resolved through prayer. Many factors can be jointly present in a single case, contributing to our internal mayhem: issues with our family of origin, biomedical factors, psychological disorders, relational tension, lifestyle issues, life stressors, unconfessed sin, and spiritual issues including demonic oppression. Therefore, it is always important to consider that a combination of multiple factors may be contributing to the upheaval in someone's life. As such, we must be integrative, careful, and holistic in our approaches, taking into consideration the interrelationships among the spiritual, personal, cultural, social, and psychological aspects of our human existence. The process toward restoration and healing may be arduous, as we live in a broken world with broken systems that constantly affect us. However, freedom can be attained as we become honest with ourselves and seek the guidance of the Spirit.

21. Nouwen, *Inner Voice*, 7.

Practical Considerations

I will close with some practical considerations with regard to spiritual warfare and its methodologies for practical ministry. First, because a fair amount of criticism has arisen around the topic of spiritual warfare, partly due to the influence of a rationalistic culture, but mostly because of the many unbalanced ideas surrounding these practices, it is important to navigate spiritual warfare with proper knowledge. We should not expect that a prayer-based freedom ministry will offer a magic pill that suddenly takes all one's ills away. Expecting long-standing issues to be rapidly resolved is not aligned with an appropriate view of the process of freedom. Discipleship is fundamental in helping individuals who have newly gained freedom as a result of an encounter with the healing grace of God to become well-grounded as Christians.

Second, a holistic, integrative, and carefully defined method will likely result in better diagnoses and outcomes. Besides the traditional power-encounter and truth-encounter approaches, a grace-encounter approach is also necessary to partner with the Holy Spirit effectively. Through this approach, individuals can release burdens, extend forgiveness, and receive the healing grace of Christ through confession and prayer. Those ministering to them must acknowledge their deep wounds and give the person the right to express and release negative emotions without blaming them or judging them for feeling those emotions. Individuals must not experience only the power of the Spirit that breaks chains, nor is an encounter with the truth of the gospel sufficient to restore one's distorted thinking. Rather, an encounter with the redemptive grace of God, extended through his body, makes it possible for one to experience deep transformation one step at a time.

Finally, the most difficult and strenuous situations in life can be managed *by* faith, although not exclusively *through* faith. In some situations, it is of absolute importance to allow professionals to be a means by which the victory of Christ can be applied and obtained. In times of tragedy, abuse, loss or neglect, the expertise of counselors and therapists can help. In times of pain, temporary relief can be obtained through the means of medicine or natural remedies. In times of relational difficulty, finding mentors who can help navigate turbulent waters is a prudent step. Living by faith does not preclude taking advantage of the expertise of the scientific community, which can aid us in the process of becoming whole and obtaining victory over our infirmities, traumatic experiences, and emotional disorders. Appropriating every possible means by which Christ's victory can be manifested on earth is a sign of wisdom, humility, and faith.

Conclusion

Our world is constantly changing, and as a result, Christians are continually challenged to think anew about their faith. Urbanization and new patterns of migration have contributed to the formation of a tapestry of cultural plurality. As a result, the social fabric of society has undergone a swift transformation, posing new opportunities for Christians to practice their faith. The last few decades have seen large multicultural populations emerge in North America as never before. The emergence of a multi-cultural and multi-religious world makes it fundamental to embody our peculiarity as the people of God. The ability and responsibility of the church to relate to the other is based on faith in a God who relates to the other. To be a Christian community is to live in fellowship with the other. Nevertheless, this relational approach should not be devoid of a presentation of the power of the gospel to transform lives.

Missional living is founded on dynamic relationships that are based on the biblical principle of love. Because God so *loved* the world, he gave and sent his Son. Because the Son so *loved* the world, he gave and sent the church. Because the church *loves* God, it gives and sends its people into the world. Jesus came to save the lost, to serve the lowly, and to send the church to do the same. This sending allows the church to serve the interests of the kingdom of God and bring people into the knowledge of his salvation. God's purposes for the world call us to be his witnesses and hosts in complex environments. We are called not only to break barriers, but to bear witness to the power of the gospel to mend broken hearts.

The evidence of our love for God is our love for neighbor. This love plays out not only within the sphere of church gatherings and its many activities, but also in workplaces, streets, markets, family rooms, and public squares, where we encounter neighbors, friends, and strangers. Missional disciples, in their daily walk with Jesus, learn to see broken and unfamiliar people, made in the image of God, as individuals in need of the light of the world—Jesus. When disciples of Christ are on mission, they become more readily aware that in helping others, we also help ourselves. As Vanderstelt says, "The ones on the mission are often more profoundly impacted than anyone else. The mission happens to them. They go to make disciples, but they are the ones who are changed while on the mission. The mission itself is God's tool for forming us."[1]

Christian mission involves building and restoring community in Christ through the power of the Spirit. Our spiritual formation becomes part of a larger project in which God invites the follower of Christ to partner with him so that the world may come to know the purposes and plans he has in store for us. By reinforcing our understanding of the *Imago Dei,* we recognize that every neighbor can help us become more like Christ as we meet him in the eyes of the other. In Zscheile's words, "It is through our encounters with strangers, especially those unlike us, that we come to know the richness of the image of God and learn new insights into the gospel."[2]

As partners in the mission of God, disciples of Christ are called to engage in God's work with intentionality and purpose. Missional disciples must be willing to move out of their places of familiarity and minister in all types of ways—relationally, dialogically, communally, and holistically. As we respond to the needs that surround us and partner with God in his redemptive work, our work will bear long-lasting fruit. Given the human tendency

1. Vanderstelt, *Saturate,* 114.

2. Zscheile, *Cultivating Sent Communities,* 20.

toward self-centeredness and ethno-centrism, we must learn to see the world with "soft eyes." In this softening, we become channels of grace into hearts that have long been captive to deceit and hopelessness.

As we gracefully activate the spiritual gifts we have received from the Father, we do it with the intention that others may come "to grasp how wide and long and high and deep is the love of Christ" for us (Eph 3:18). Our own journey into the depths of God's love will become the necessary catalyst for breaking barriers in a diverse and fractured world. The experience and expression of deep spiritual healing and transformation demonstrated by Christians is something our churches and world need to see today.

In a complex, diverse, and fragmented world, our call is not to be at home in the church, but to become pilgrims on a journey toward the realization of the kingdom. As a result, we must seek to continually love and care for our neighbor. The fact that human beings have been created in the image of God presents wide-ranging implications for loving and honoring one another. When assumptions about the other are dismantled and redirected, Christians can stand in the gap through prayer and seek intentional relationships across lines of difference. In so doing, we might find a way into a world that desperately needs to hear the good news of Jesus Christ.

God is continually calling us to a project of deconstruction and reconstruction. The deconstruction happens when we break down walls of division and fences of hostility that have separated us from each other. The reconstruction takes place when we build paths to connect with others as witnesses of the transformative power of the gospel. Perhaps, as we travel along the narrow road of obedience, the walls we have stealthily constructed around our "city on a hill" will be broken down for all to see the glory of our King—a King who is worthy to be worshipped for all eternity.

Bibliography

Adedibu, Babatunde Aderimi. "Reverse Mission or Migrant Sanctuaries? Migration, Symbolic Mapping, and Missionary Challenges of Britain's Black Majority Churches." *Pneuma* 35 (2013) 405–23.

Ajani, Ezekiel. "Migration and Mission: An Exploration of the Mission Understanding and Activities of the Redeemed Christian Church of God." PhD diss., Trinity International University, 2016.

Allbee, Rick. "Christ Witnessing to Culture: Toward a New Paradigm Between Christ and Culture." *Stone-Campbell* 8 (2005) 17–33.

Ammerman, Nancy Tatum. *Congregation and Community.* New Brunswick, NJ: Rutgers University Press, 1997.

Anderson, Neil T. *The Bondage Breaker.* Eugene, OR: Harvest House, 2019.

———. *Ten Steps to Freedom in Christ.* Minneapolis: Bethany House, 2014.

———. *Victory Over the Darkness: Realize the Power of Your Identity in Christ.* Minneapolis: Bethany House, 2000.

Anderson, Neil T., and Timothy M. Warner. *The Essential Guide to Spiritual Warfare.* Grand Rapids: Bethany House, 2000.

Appleby, David W. *It's Only a Demon: A Model of Christian Deliverance.* 2nd ed. Goode, VA: Spiritual Interventions, 2017.

Arndt, W., F. W. Danker, and W. Bauer. *A Greek-English Lexicon of the New Testament and Other Early Christian Literature.* 3rd ed. Chicago: University of Chicago Press, 2000.

Arnold, Clinton E. *3 Crucial Questions about Spiritual Warfare.* Grand Rapids: Baker Academic, 1997.

———. *Powers of Darkness: Principalities and Powers in Paul's Letters.* Downers Grove, IL: InterVarsity, 1992.

Asamoha-Gyadu, Kwabena. "An African Pentecostal on Mission in Eastern Europe: The Church of the 'Embassy of God' in the Ukraine." *Pneuma* 27 (2005) 297–321.

Bakker, Janel Kragt. *Sister Churches: American Congregations and Their Partners Abroad.* New York: Oxford University Press, 2014.

Barder, Owen. "What Is Poverty Reduction?" Center for Global Development Working Paper 170 (2009) 1–24.

Bibliography

Bauckham, Richard J. *Jesus and the Eyewitnesses: The Gospels as Eyewitness Testimony.* Grand Rapids: Eerdmans, 2006.

Birth, Kevin. "What Is Your Mission Here? A Trinidadian Perspective on Visits from the "Church of Disneyworld." *Missiology: An International Review* 34 (2006) 497–508.

Beard, Christopher. "Missional Discipleship: Discerning Spiritual-Formation Practices and Goals Within the Missional Movement." *Missiology: An International Review* 43 (2015) 175–94.

Beilby, James K., and Paul R. Eddy, eds. *Understanding Spiritual Warfare: Four Views.* Grand Rapids: Baker Academic, 2012.

Benthal, Jonathan. "R20: the G20 Religion Forum led by Indonesia." Obsreligion. cnrs.fr, 2023. https://obsreligion.cnrs.fr/bulletin/r20-the-g20-religion-forum-led-by-indonesia-english-version/.

Bevans, Stephen B. "A Prophetic Dialogue Approach." In *The Mission of the Church,* edited by Craig Ott, 3–20. Grand Rapids: Baker Academic, 2016.

Bloesch, Donald G. *The Holy Spirit: Works and Gifts.* Downers Grove, IL: InterVarsity, 2000.

Bonhoeffer, Dietrich. *The Cost of Discipleship.* New York: Touchstone, 2018.

———. *Life Together: The Classic Exploration of Christian Community.* New York: Harper One, 1954.

Borthwick, Paul. *Western Christians in Global Mission: What's the Role of the American Church?* Downers Grove, IL: InterVarsity, 2012.

Bourdieu, Pierre. "The Forms of Capital." In *The Handbook of Theory and Research for the Sociology of Education,* edited by John G. Richardson, 241–58. New York: Greenwood, 1986.

Boyd, Gregory. *God at War: The Bible and Spiritual Conflict.* Downers Grove, IL: InterVarsity, 1997.

Breen, Mike. *Building a Discipling Culture: How to Release a Missional Movement by Discipling People like Jesus Did.* Pawleys Island, SC: 3DM, 2011.

———. "Why the Missional Movement Will Fail." *Verge,* September 14, 2011, http://www.vergenetwork.org/2011/09/14/mike-breen-why-the-missional-movement-will-fail.

Brown, C. M. "Friendship is Forever: Congregation-to-Congregation Relationships." In *Effective Engagement in Short-Term Missions: Doing It Right!* edited by Robert J. Priest, 209–37. Pasadena, CA: William Carey Library, 2008.

Brown, Rebecca. *He Came to Set the Captives Free.* New Kensington, PA: Whitaker House, 1992.

Brown, Rebecca, and Daniel Yoder. *Unbroken Curses.* New Kensington, PA: Whitaker House, 1995.

Brueggemann, Walter. *Israel's Praise: Doxology Against Idolatry and Ideology.* Philadelphia, PA: Fortress, 1988.

———. *The Prophetic Imagination.* Minneapolis: Fortress, 2001.

Burge, Ryan P. *The Nones: Where They Came From, Who They Are, and Where They Are Going.* Minneapolis: Fortress, 2021.

Bibliography

Burning Man. "What Is Burning Man? The Ten Principles of Burning Man." http://burningman.org/culture/philosophical-center/10-principles/.

Burt, Roland. *Structural Holes*. Cambridge, MA: Harvard University Press, 1992.

Campese, Gioacchino. "The Irruption of Migrants: Theology of Migration in the 21st Century." *Theological Studies* 73 (2012) 3–14.

Clark, Randy and Mary Healy. *The Spiritual Gifts Handbook*. Minneapolis: Chosen, 2018.

Clarke, Clifton. "Dialogue or Diatribe: Toward a Renewal Approach to Interreligious Conversation." In *Global Renewal, Religious Pluralism, and the Great Commission,* edited by Amos Yong and Clifton Clarke, 17–42. Lexington, KY: Emeth, 2011.

Corbertt, Steve, and Brian Fikkert. *When Helping Hurts: How to Alleviate Poverty Without Hurting the Poor. . . and Yourself.* Chicago: Moody, 2012.

Cohen, Robin. *Global Diasporas: An Introduction*. New York: Routledge, 2023.

Coleman, James S. "Social Capital in the Creation of Human Capital." *American Journal of Sociology* 94 (1988) 95–120.

Cox, Daniel A. "Generation Z and the Future of Faith in America." American Survey Center, 2022, https://www.americansurveycenter.org/research/generation-z-future-of-faith/.

Cronshaw, Darren, and Rosemary Dewerse. *We Are Pilgrims: Mission from, in, and with the Margins of Our Diverse World.* Victoria, Australia: UNOH, 2015.

Cross, Terry. *The People of God's Presence: An Introduction to Ecclesiology.* Grand Rapids: Baker Academic, 2019.

———. *Serving the People of God's Presence.* Grand Rapids: Baker Academic, 2020.

Crouch, Andy. "Unexpected Global Lessons." *Christianity Today* 51 (2007) 30–33.

Cueva, Samuel. *Mission Partnership in Creative Tension*. Cumbria, UK: Langham, 2015.

Cyprian of Carthage. "The Unity of the Catholic Church." In Robert L. Ferm, *Readings in the History of Christian Thought.* New York: Holt, Reinhart and Winston, 1964.

De La Torre, Miguel A. *The U.S. Immigration Crisis: Toward and Ethics of Place.* Eugene, OR: Wipf and Stock, 2016.

De Witte, Melissa. "Gen Z are not 'Coddled.'" *Stanford News*, 2002, https://news.stanford.edu/2022/01/03/know-gen-z/.

DeYoung, Curtiss Paul, et al. *United by Faith: The Multiracial Congregation as an Answer to the Problem of Race.* Oxford: Oxford University Press, 2003.

Dow, Jasmine. "Where the Margins Meet: An Exploration of the Prophetic Dimensions of a Church Willing to Embrace." In *We Are Pilgrims*, edited by Darren Cronshaw and Rosemary Dewerse, 139–50. Victoria, Australia: UNOH, 2015.

Driver, John. *Images of the Church in Mission*. Harrisonburg, VA: Herald, 1997.

Duke, David N. "Giving Voice to Suffering in Worship: A Study in the Theodicies of Hymnody." *Encounter* 52 (1991) 263–72.

Dulles, Avery. *Models of the Church.* New York: Doubleday, 2002.

Edwards, Jonathan. "The Excellency of Christ." https://www.ccel.org/ccel/edwards/sermons.excellency.html

Ellis, G. "The Dimensions of Poverty." *Springer* 15 (1984) 229–53.

Emerson, Michael D., and Christian Smith. *Divided by Faith: Evangelical Religion and the Problem of Race in America.* Oxford: Oxford University Press, 2000.

Escobar, Samuel. *The New Global Mission: The Gospel from Everywhere to Everyone.* Downers Grove, IL: InterVarsity, 2003.

Ferguson, Everett. *Images of the Church in Mission.* Grand Rapids: Eerdmans, 1996.

Ferm, Deane William. *Third World Liberation Theologies.* Maryknoll, NY: Orbis, 1986.

Flemming, Dean. *Recovering the Full Mission of God.* Downers Grove, IL: InterVarsity, 2013.

Friedman, Edwin H. *A Failure of Nerve.* New York: Seabury, 2007.

Gagnon, Robert A.J. *The Bible and Homosexual Practice: Texts and Hermeneutics.* Nashville: Abingdon, 2002.

George, Sam, and Miriam Adeney, eds. *Refugee Diaspora: Missions amid the Greatest Humanitarian Christ of our Times.* Littleton, CO: William Carey, 2018.

Giddens, Anthony. *Modernity and Self-Identity: Self and Society in the Late Modern Age.*

Stanford, CA: Stanford University Press, 1991.

Gillmor, D. *We the Media: Grassroots Journalism by the People, for the People.* Sebastopol, CA: O'Reilly, 2004.

Gittel, Ross, and Vidal Avis. *Community Organizing: Building Social Capital as a Development Strategy.* Thousand Oaks, CA: Sage, 1998.

Gittins, Anthony J. *Ministry at the Margins: Strategy and Spirituality for Mission.* Maryknoll, NY: Orbis, 2022.

Global Gates. "Gateway City: New York City." Globalgates.info, 2023. https://globalgates.info/gateway-city/new-york-city/.

Goheen, Michael W. *A Light to the Nations.* Grand Rapids: Baker Academic, 2011.

————. *The Church and Its Vocation: Lesslie Newbigin's Missionary Ecclesiology.* Grand Rapids: Baker Academic, 2018.

Gort, Jerald D. "The Search for Interreligious Coivance, Ongoing Challenge and Charge." *Verbum et Ecclesia* 29 (2008) 758–61.

Graeff, Peter. "Social Capital: The Dark Side." In *Handbook of Social Capital: The Troika of Sociology, Political Science, and Economics,* edited by Gert T. Svensen and Gunnar Lind Svensen, 143–61. Northampton, MA: Edward Elgar, 2010.

Granovetter, Mark S. "The Strength of Weak Ties." *American Journal of Sociology* 78 (1973) 1360–80.

Guder, Darrell, ed. *Missional Church: A Vision for the Sending of the Church in North America.* Grand Rapids: Eerdmans, 1998.

Gushee, David P. *The Sacredness of Human Life: Why an Ancient Biblical Vision Is Key to the World's Future.* Grand Rapids: Eerdmans, 2013.

Gustafson, James M. "Ways of Using Scripture." In *From Christ to the World,* edited by Wayne Boulton et al., 21–26. Grand Rapids: Eerdmans, 1994.

Halter, Hugh, and Matt Smay. *And: The Gathered and Scattered Church.* Grand Rapids: Zondervan, 2010.

Hanifan, Lyda J. "Appalachia: The Rural School Community Center." *Annals of American Academy of Political and Social Science* 67 (1916) 130–38.

Harper, Brad, and Paul Louis Metzger. *The Church of Christ: A Biblical Ecclesiology for Today.* Grand Rapids: Brazos, 2009.

Hefferan, Tara. *Twinning Faith and Development: Catholic Parish Partnering in the US and Haiti.* Bloomfield, CT: Kumarian, 2007.

Hick, John H. *An Interpretation of Religion.* New Haven, CT: Yale University Press, 1989.

Hiebert, Paul G. *Anthropological Insights for Missionaries.* Grand Rapids: Baker Academic, 1985.

———. "The Flaw of the Excluded Middle." *Missiology: An International Review* 10 (1982) 35–47.

Hofstede, Geert, et al. *Cultures and Organizations: Software of the Mind.* New York: McGraw Hill, 2010.

Hollinger, Dennis P. *Choosing the Good: Christian Ethics in a Complex World.* Grand Rapids: Baker Academic, 2002.

Horrobin, Peter. *Healing Through Deliverance.* Grand Rapids: Chosen, 2008.

Hout, Michael, and Claude S. Fischer. "Why More Americans Have No Religious Preference:

Politics and Generations." *American Sociological Review* 67 (2002) 165–90.

Howard, Tim, and Brian Burke. *With Gentle Authority: A Manual for Inner Healing and Freedom Ministry.* Nashville: NCW, 2016.

Jacobs, Jane. *The Death and Life of Great American Cities: The Failure of Town Planning.* New York: Random House, 1960.

Johnstone, Patrick. "People Groups: How Many Unreached?" *International Journal of Frontier Missions* 7 (1990) 35–40.

Jones, Beth Felker. *Faithful: A Theology of Sex.* Grand Rapids: Zondervan, 2015.

Katz, Roberta, et al. *Gen Z, Explained: The Art of Living in a Digital Age.* Chicago: University of Chicago Press, 2021.

Keener, Craig. *Miracles Today: The Supernatural Work of God in the Modern World.* Grand Rapids: Baker Academic, 2021.

———. "Spirit Possession as a Cross-Cultural Experience." *Bulletin for Biblical Research* 20 (2010) 215–36.

Kim, Hun. "Receiving Mission: Reflection on Reversed Phenomena in Mission by Migrant Workers from Global Churches." *Transformation* 28 (2011) 62–67.

King, Martin Luther Jr. *A Gift of Love.* Boston, MA: Beacon, 1981.

———. *The Measure of a Man.* Bensenville, IL: Lushena, 2013.

Kirk, J. Andrew. *What Is Mission? Theological Explorations.* Minneapolis: Fortress, 2000.

Knitter, Paul F. "Interreligious Dialogue: What? Why? How?" In *Interreligious Dialogue: An Anthology of Voices Bridging Cultural and Religious Divides,* edited by Christoffer Grundmann, 25–35. Winona, MN: Anselm Academic, 2015.

Kraft, Charles H. *Defeating Dark Angels: Breaking Demonic Oppression in the Believer's Life.* Minneapolis: Chosen, 1992.

———. *Two Hours of Freedom: A Simple and Effective Model for Healing and Deliverance.* Grand Rapids: Chosen, 2010.

Kraft, Marguerite G. *Understanding Spiritual Power: A Forgotten Dimension of Cross-Cultural Mission and Ministry.* Eugene, OR: Wipf and Stock, 1995.

Kreider, Alan, and Eleanor Kreider. *Worship and Mission after Christendom.* Harrisonburg, VA: Herald, 2011.

Lausanne Movement. "The Cape Town Commitment." October 2010, www.lausanne.org/content/ctcommitment.

———. "Lausanne Covenant." 1974, http://www.lausanne.org/content/covenant/lausanne-covenant.

Lederleitner, Mary T. *Cross-Cultural Partnerships: Navigating the Complexities of Money and Mission.* Downers Grove, IL: InterVarsity, 2010.

Lee, Peter T., and James Sung-Hwan Park. "Beyond People Group Thinking: A Critical Reevaluation of Unreached People Groups." *Missiology: An International Review* 46 (2018) 212–25.

Lewis, C. S. *The Great Divorce.* New York: HarperCollins, 1973.

———. *Mere Christianity.* New York: Macmillan, 1978.

Lim, Chaeyoon, Carol Ann MacGregor, and Robert D. Putnam. "Secular and Liminal: Discovering Heterogeneity among Religious Nones." *Journal for the Scientific Study of Religion* 49 (2010) 596–618.

Lin, Nan. *Social Capital: A Theory of Social Structure and Action.* Cambridge: Cambridge University Press, 2001.

Lipka, Michael, and Claire Gecewicz. "More Americans Now Say They're Spiritual but Not Religious." Pew Research Center, September 6, 2017, https://www.pewresearch.org/fact-tank/2017/09/06/more-americans-now-say-theyre-spiritual-but-not-religious/.

Littau, Jeremy. "The Virtual Social Capital of Online Communities." Ph.D. diss., University of Missouri, 2009.

MacNutt, Francis. *Deliverance from Evil Spirits: A Practical Manual.* Grand Rapids: Chosen, 1995.

Macquarrie, John. *Principles of Christian Theology.* 2nd ed. London, UK: Pearson, 1977.

McDermott, Gerald R., and Harold A. Netland. *A Trinitarian Theology of Religions: An Evangelical Proposal.* Oxford: Oxford University Press, 2014.

McGavran, Donald A., and Peter C. Wagner. *Understanding Church Growth.* Grand Rapids: Eerdmans, 1990.

McGrath, Alister. *Christian Theology: An Introduction.* Malden, MA: John Wiley & Sons, 2015.

McQuilkin, Robertson. "Stop Sending Money! Breaking the Cycle of Missions Dependency." *Christianity Today* 43 (1999) 57–59.

Miles, Rebekah L. *The Pastor as Moral Guide.* Minneapolis: Fortress, 1999.

Moltmann, Jürgen. *The Church in the Power of the Spirit.* New York: Harper & Row, 1977.

———. *The Spirit of Life: A Universal Affirmation.* Minneapolis: Fortress, 2001.

Moodie, Ellen. "Inequality and Intimacy Between Sister Communities in El Salvador and the United States." *Missiology: An International Review* 41 (2013) 146–62.

Moreau, A. Scott. *Essentials of Spiritual Warfare: Equipped to Win the Battle.* Wheaton, IL: Harold Shaw, 1997.

Moreau, A. Scott, et al., eds. *Deliver Us from Evil: An Uneasy Frontier in Christian Mission.* Monrovia, CA: MARC World Vision, 2002.

Muck, Terry C. "Interreligious Dialogue: Conversations That Enable Christian Witness." *International Bulletin of Missionary Research* 35 (2011) 188–94.

Mulholland, Robert Jr. *Invitation to a Journey: A Road Map for Spiritual Formation.* Downers Grove, IL: InterVarsity, 2016.

Murphy, Ed. *The Handbook for Spiritual Warfare.* Nashville: Thomas Nelson, 1992.

Muto, Susan. "Living Contemplatively and Serving God in the World: Two Sides of the Coin in Christian Ministry." *Journal of Spiritual Formation & Soul Care* 6 (2013) 82–92.

Nagel, Thomas. *The View from Nowhere.* New York: Oxford University Press, 1989.

Nash, Ronald. *Is Jesus the Only Way?* Grand Rapids: Zondervan, 1994.

Netland, Harold. *Dissonant Voices: Religious Pluralism and the Question of Truth.* Grand Rapids: Eerdmans, 1991.

Newbigin, Lesslie. *Mission in Christ's Way: Bible Studies.* Geneva: WCC Publications, 1987.

———. *The Open Secret.* Grand Rapids: Eerdmans, 1995.

Noble, T. A. *Holy Trinity: Holy People.* Eugene, OR: Cascade, 2013.

Nouwen, Henri J. *The Inner Voice of Love.* New York: Image Books, 1999.

———. *Spiritual Formation: Following the Movements of the Spirit.* New York: HarperOne, 2010.

———. *Turn My Mourning into Dancing; Finding Hope in Hard Times.* Nashville: Thomas Nelson, 2001.

———. *The Wounded Healer: Ministry in Contemporary Society.* New York: Doubleday, 1979.

Nouwen, Henri J., Donald P. McNeill, and Douglas A. Morrison. *Compassion: A Reflection on the Christian Life*. New York: Image, 1982.

Olmstead, Gracy. "Why Millennials Long for Liturgy." *American Conservative* 13 (2014) 7–9.

Olukoya, D. K. *Deliverance from Triangular Powers*. Lagos, Nigeria: Mountain of Fire and Miracles Ministries, 2013.

Offutt, Stephen. *New Centers of Global Evangelicalism in Latin America and Africa*. New York: Cambridge University Press, 2015.

Oden, Thomas C. *Classic Christianity: A Systematic Theology*. New York: HarperOne, 1992.

Ott, Craig. "Missions and Money: Revisiting Pauline Practices and Principles." *Evangelical Review of Theology* 42 (2018) 4–20.

Ott, Craig, ed. *The Mission of the Church: Five Views in Conversation*. Grand Rapids: Baker Academic, 2016.

Ott, Craig, et al. *Encountering Theology of Mission*. Grand Rapids: Baker Academic, 2010.

Payne, J.D. *Strangers Next Door: Immigration, Migration and Mission*. Downers Grove, IL: InterVarsity, 2012.

Peretti, Frank. *Piercing the Darkness*. Wheaton, IL: Crossway, 1989.

———. *This Present Darkness*. Wheaton, IL: Crossway, 1986.

Pettigrew, Thomas F. "Intergroup Contact Theory." *Annual Review of Psychology* 49 (1998) 65–85.

Pettigrew, Thomas F. and Linda R. Tropp. "A Meta-Analytic Test of Intergroup Contact Theory." *Journal of Personality and Social Psychology* 90 (2006) 751–83.

Pew Research Center. "America's Changing Religious Landscape." May 12, 2015 http://www.pewforum.org/2015/05/12/americas-changing-religious-landscape/.

———. "'Nones' on the Rise." October 9, 2012, http://www.pewforum.org/2012/10/09/nones-on-the-rise/.

———. "Why America's 'Nones' Don't Identify with a Religion." August 8, 2018, https://www.pewresearch.org/fact-tank/2018/08/08/why-americas-nones-dont-identify-with-a-religion/.

Pettigrew, Thomas F. "Intergroup Contact Theory." *Annual Review of Psychology* 49 (1998) 65–85.

Pinnock, Clark. *Flame of Love: A Theology of the Holy Spirit*. Downers Grove, IL: InterVarsity, 1996.

———. *A Wideness in God's Mercy*. Grand Rapids: Zondervan, 1992.

Pitman, David. *Twentieth Century Christian Responses to Religious Pluralism*. London: Routledge, 2014.

Plueddemann, James E. *Leading Across Cultures*. Downers Grove, IL: InterVarsity, 2009.

Pocock, Michael, et al. *The Changing Face of World Missions: Engaging Contemporary Issues and Trends*. Grand Rapids: Baker Academic, 2005.

Pohl, Christine D. *Living into Community*. Grand Rapids: Eerdmans, 2012.

Pope, Francis, and Ahmad Al-Tayyeb. "A Document on Human Fraternity For World Peace and Living Together." Vatican.va, 2019. https://www.vatican.va/content/francesco/en/travels/2019/outside/documents/papa-francesco_20190204_documento-fratellanza-umana.html.

Portes, Alejandro. "The Two Meanings of Social Capital." *Sociological Forum* 15 (2000) 1–12.

Priest, Robert J. "Peruvian Churches Acquire Linking Social Capital Through STM Partnerships." *Journal of Latin American Theology* 2 (2007) 175–89.

Prill, Thorsten. *Global Mission on Our Doorstep: Forced Migration and the Future of the Church.* Nordertstedt, Germany: Grin, 2017.

Putnam, Robert D. *Bowling Alone: The Collapse and Revival of American Community.*
New York: Simon and Schuster, 2000.

———. *Making Democracy Work: Civic Traditions in Modern Italy.* Princeton, NJ: Princeton University Press, 1993.

Putnam, Robert D., and David E. Campbell: *American Grace: How Religion Divides and Unites Us.* New York: Simon and Schuster, 2010.

Putnam, Robert D., and Lewis M. Feldstein. *Better Together: Restoring the American Community.* New York: Simon and Schuster, 2004.

Rah, Soon-Chan. *The Next Evangelicalism: Freeing the Church from Western Cultural Captivity.* Downers Grove, IL: InterVarsity, 2009.

Rahner, Karl. *Spirit in the World.* London: Sheed and Ward, 1968.

Rauschenbusch, Walter. *A Theology for the Social Gospel.* Edinburgh: CrossReach, 2017.

Reddish, Mitchell. *Revelation.* Macon, GA: Smyth and Helwys, 2001.

Riccardi, Andrea. *To the Margins: Pope Francis and the Mission of the Church.* Maryknoll, NY: Orbis, 2018.

Rickett, Daniel. "Walk With me: the Path of Interdependency." *Evangelical Missions Quarterly* 48 (2012) 162–68.

Ricoeur, Paul. *Oneself as Another.* Chicago: University of Chicago Press, 1992.

Roberts, Dana L. *Faithful Friendships: Embracing Diversity in Christian Community.* Grand Rapids: Eerdmans, 2019.

Rowell, John. *To Give or not to Give?* Atlanta: Authentic, 2006.

Ruspini, Elizabetta. *An Introduction to Longitudinal Research.* Routledge: New York, 2002.

Sanford, Agnes. *The Healing Gifts of the Spirit.* New York: HarperCollins, 1984.

———. *The Healing Light.* Oxford: Benediction Classics, 2017.

Sanders, Oswald J. *The Holy Spirit and His Gifts.* Grand Rapids: Zondervan, 1972.

Sandford, John Loren, and Mark Sandford. *Deliverance and Inner Healing.* Grand Rapids: Chosen, 1992.

Schenck-Fontaine, Anika, and Lidia Panico. "Many Kinds of Poverty: Three Dimensions of Economic Hardship, Their Combinations, and Children's Behavior Problems." *Demography* 56 (2019) 2279–2305.

Schroeder, Roger. "Proclamation and Interreligious Dialogue as Prophetic Dialogue." *Missiology: An International Review* 41 (2013) 56–62.

Schwartz, Glenn J. "Cutting the Apron Strings." *Evangelical Missions Quarterly* 30 (1991) 36–43.

———. *When Charity Destroys Dignity: Overcoming Unhealthy Dependency in the Christian Movement.* Bloomington, IN: Author House, 2007.

Seamands, David. *Healing for Damaged Emotions.* Colorado Springs: David Cook, 2015.

———. *Wounds That Heal: Bringing Your Hurts to the Cross.* Downers Grove, IL: InterVarsity, 2003.

Seversen, Beth. *Not Done Yet: Reaching and Keeping Unchurched Emerging Adults.* Downers Grove: InterVarsity, 2020.

Shenk, David. "The Gospel of Reconciliation within the Wrath of Nations." *International Bulletin of Mission Research* 32 (2008) 3–11.

Shields, T. T. *Christ in the Old Testament: How to Find Christ in Bible Study.* Scottdale, PA: Gospel Witness, 1972.

Shirer, Priscilla. *The Prince Warriors.* Nashville: B&H, 2016.

Singarayar, John. "Social Media and the Church's Mission." *Vidyajyoti Journal of Theological Reflection* 83 (2019) 791–95.

Smith, Gregory A. "About Three-in-Ten U.S. Adults Are Now Religiously Unaffiliated." Pew Research Center, 2021, https://www.pewresearch.org/religion/2021/12/14/about-three-in-ten-u-s-adults-are-now-religiously-unaffiliated/.

Sorens, Matthew, and Jenny Hwang. *Welcoming the Stranger: Justice, Compassion and Truth in the Immigration Debate.* Downers Grove, IL: InterVarsity, 2018.

Stark, Jeff. *The News Is Good.* Kansas City, MO: The Foundry, 2023.

Stott, John. *Christian Mission in the Modern World.* Downers Grove, IL: InterVarsity, 1975.

———. *The Radical Disciple.* Downers Grove, IL: InterVarsity, 2010.

Stott, John, and Christopher Wright. *Christian Mission in the Modern World.* Downers Grove, IL: InterVarsity, 2015.

Swidler, Leonard, Khalid Duran, and Reuven Firestone. *Trialogue: Jews, Christians, and Muslims in Dialogue.* New London, CT: Twenty-Third, 2007.

Tennent, Timothy. *The Call to Holiness.* Franklin, TN: Seedbed, 2014.

———. *Christianity at the Religious Roundtable.* Grand Rapids: Baker Academic, 2002.

———. *For the Body: Recovering a Theology of Gender, Sexuality, and the Human Body.* Grand Rapids: Zondervan, 2021.

———. *Invitation to World Missions: A Trinitarian Missiology for the Twenty-First Century.* Grand Rapids: Kregel, 2010.

———. "The Millennials are Coming!" Seedbed (blog), Asbury Theological Seminary, 2015, http://timothytennent.com/2015/01/14/the-millennials-are-coming/.

Tira, Sadri Joy, and Tetsunao Yamamori, eds. *Scattered and Gathered: A Global Compendium of Diaspora Missiology.* Carlisle, Cumbria, UK: Langham, 2020.

Tizon, Al. *Whole and Reconciled: Gospel, Church, and Mission in a Fractured World.* Grand Rapids: Baker Academic, 2018.

Turnau, Ted. *Popologetics: Popular Culture in Christian Perspective.* Phillipsburg, NJ: P&R, 2012.

Turner, Victor. *The Ritual Process Structure and Anti-Structure.* Piscataway, NJ: Transaction, 1995.

Twibell, Simone. "Interreligious Dialogue: Towards an Evangelical Approach." *Evangelical Review of Theology* 44 (2020) 266–79.

———. "Reversing the Flow of Short-Term Missions Within a Partnership Model: Perceptual Outcomes." *Missiology: An International Review* 49 (2020) 176–88.

———. "Social Capital and the Church: Engaging Virtually for the Sake of the World." *International Bulletin of Missionary Research* 46 (2021) 1–8.

———. "Strategic-Level Spiritual Warfare: An Assessment of Its Premises and Practices." *Mediator* 15 (2020) 83–110.

Twenge, Jean M. "Generational and Time Period Differences in American Adolescents' Religious Orientation, 1966–2014." *Plus One* 10 (2015) 1–17.

Twenge, Jean M., et al. "Age, Period, and Cohort Trends in Mood Disorder Indicators and Suicide-Related Outcomes in a Nationally Representative Dataset, 2005–2017." *Journal of Abnormal Psychology* 128 (2019) 185–99.

Van Engen, Charles E. "The Glocal Church: Locality and Catholicity in a Globalizing World." In *Globalizing Theology: Belief and Practice in an Era of World Christianity,* edited by Craig Ott and Harold A. Netland, 157–79. Grand Rapids: Baker Academic, 2006.

Vanderstelt, Jeff. *Saturate: Being Disciples of Jesus in the Everyday Stuff of Life.* Wheaton, IL: Crossway, 2015.

Vaughan, Joy. *Phenomenal Phenomena: Biblical and Multicultural Accounts of Spirits and Exorcism.* Waco, TX: Baylor University, 2023.

Volf, Miroslav. *After Our Likeness.* Grand Rapids: Eerdmans, 1998.

———. *Exclusion and Embrace.* Nashville: Abingdon, 2019.

———. "Soft Difference: Theological Reflections on the Relation Between Church and Culture in 1 Peter." *Ex Auditu* (1994) 15–30.

Wan, Enoch. *Diaspora Missiology: Theory, Methodology, and Practice.* Portland, OR: Institute of Diaspora Studies, 2011.

Wardle, Terry. *Strong Winds & Crashing Waves: Meeting Jesus in the Memories of Traumatic Events.* Abilene, TX: Leafwood, 2007.

———. *Wounded: How to Find Wholeness and Inner Healing in Christ.* Abilene, TX: Leafwood, 2005.

Wellman, B., et al. "Computer Networks as Social Networks: Collaborative Work, Telework, and Virtual Community." *Annual Review of Sociology* 22 (1996) 213–38.

Wesley, David. *A Common Mission: Healthy Patterns in Congregational Mission Partnerships.* Eugene, OR: Wipf & Stock, 2014.

Wesley, John. "Cause of the Inefficacy of Christianity." *The Sermons of John Wesley.* Wesley Center Online. http://wesley.nnu.edu/john-wesley/the-sermons-of-john-wesley-1872-edition/sermon-116-causes-of-the-inefficacy-of-christianity.

———. "On Sin in Believers." *The Sermons of John Wesley.* Wesley Center Online. http://wesley.nnu.edu/john-wesley/the-sermons-of-john-wesley-1872-edition/sermon-13-on-sin-in-believers/.

———. "The Scripture Way of Salvation." *The Sermons of John Wesley.* Wesley Center Online. http://wesley.nnu.edu/john-wesley/the-sermons-of-john-wesley-1872-edition/sermon-43-the-scripture-way-of-salvation/.

White, James. *Meet Generation Z: Understanding and Reaching the New Post-Christian World.* Grand Rapids: Baker, 2017.

———. *The Rise of the Nones: Understanding and Reaching the Religiously Unaffiliated.* Grand Rapids: Baker, 2004.

White, Tom. *A Believer's Guide to Spiritual Warfare.* Ventura, CA: Regal, 1990.

White, P., et al. "A Missional Study of the Use of Social Media (Facebook) by Some Ghanaian Pentecostal Pastors." *Bulletin for Christian Scholarship* 81 (2016) 1–8.

Willard, Dallas. *The Divine Conspiracy.* New York: HarperCollins, 2014.

Williams, Paul S. *Exiles on Mission.* Grand Rapids: Brazos, 2020.

Wink, Walter. *Naming the Powers: The Language of Power in the New Testament.* Philadelphia: Fortress, 1984.

Winter, Ralph D., and Bruce A. Koch. "Finishing the Task: The Unreached Peoples Challenge." *International Journal of Frontier Missions* 19 (2002) 15–25.

Wolff, Hans Walter. "The Kerygma of the Yahwist." Translated by Wilbur A. Benware. *Interpretation* 20 (1996) 131–58.

Woodberry, Dudley J. "Terrorism, Islam, and Mission: Reflections of a Guest in Muslim Lands." *International Bulletin of Missionary Research* 26 (2002) 5–14.

Woolcock, Michael. "Social Capital and Economic Development: Toward a Theoretical Synthesis and Policy Framework." *Theory and Society* 27 (1998) 151–208.

Woolcock, Michael, and Deepa Narayan. "Social capital: Implications for Development Theory, Research, and Policy." *World Bank Research Observer* 15 (2000) 225–49.

Wright, Christopher. *Salvation Belongs to Our God: Celebrating the Bible's Central Story.* Downers Grove: IVP, 2008.

Wuthnow, Robert. *Boundless Faith: The Global Outreach of American Churches.* Berkeley: University of California Press, 2009.

———. *Loose Connections.* Cambridge, MA: Harvard University Press, 2002.

———. "Religious Involvement and Status-Bridging Social Capital." *Journal for the Social Scientific Study of Religion* 41 (2002) 669–84.

Bibliography

———. *Saving America? Faith-Based Services and the Future of Civil Society.* Princeton, NJ: Princeton University Press, 2004.

Wuthnow, Robert, and Stephen Offutt. "Transnational Religious Connections." *Sociology of Religion* 69 (2008) 209–32.

Yarhouse, Mark, and Olya Zaporozhets. *Costly Obedience: What We Can Learn From the Celibate Gay Christian Community.* Grand Rapids: Zondervan, 2019.

Yun, Christopher. *Holy Sexuality and the Gospel: Sex, Desire, and Relationships Shaped by God's Grand Story.* New York: Multnomah, 2018.

Zscheile, Dwight J. "A Missional Theology of Spiritual Formation." In *Cultivating Sent Communities*, edited by Dwight J. Zscheile. Grand Rapids: Eerdmans, 2012.

www.ingramcontent.com/pod-product-compliance
Lightning Source LLC
Chambersburg PA
CBHW070740030726
47601CB00001B/85